Life

on the

Line

Life

on the

Line

Lauren Roche

Published by
ZYMURGY PUBLISHING
NEWCASTLE UPON TYNE

© Great Britain & Ireland 2002

ISBN 1-903506-05-0

Printed by BookMarque Limited, Croydon, UK.

Contents

Dedication

This book is for 'The Farty Family' - Maania, Paulie, Gemma, Adam and the others. May your bums never seize up.

A special dedication to Amy Morgan aged 9, who wants to be a doctor and a writer too. I hope she does it the 'proper' way.

Also for Leanne Hall, Wayne, Trevor L and Steve, Jan, Trish McQueen, Moira and Rick, Trevor T, Deirdre and Doug, Sharon and Allan, Dawn and Mac, Dirty Denis, the Hayes family, the Adams family, all my godchildren, Barbie in all her guises, and my exceedingly sexy mate Tax.

Live long.

♥ Special thanks to: Virginia and Kim Turner; everyone who enjoyed *Bent*, especially those who shared their own stories with me; Roger Whelan, Jo McMullan and Lorraine Kearns at Steele Roberts; Amanda Millar and her crew from TV3's 20/20 programme; Ian Greig and Jim Simpson; my sisters, Tracey and Shelley; my sons, Chris and Paul.

The names of some people and places have been changed for legal or privacy reasons.

Author's note

Bent not Broken, the story of my life until I graduated as a doctor at age 31, was published on my 38th birthday on 5 November 1999. The book was launched to the accompaniment of a fireworks display that the Wellington City Council put on just for me. Or so it seemed…

I wrote *Bent* to try and figure myself out in the aftermath of a failed suicide attempt. It began life in an exercise book, written longhand, in the form of a letter to my lover at the time. The first words were '*Who Am I?*' After a few false starts the writing began to flow. There were many tears and fraught nights as the story emerged. Things I'd kept secret were exposed to the page, and once there sometimes seemed to lose their power. As I wrote about my mother, she became more real; more rounded. I remembered positive things about her; fun we'd had together. Before this my memories had been the sad and angry ones of a hurt child. Bringing Mum back to life like this gave me a sense of peace. I began to understand her as an adult with problems, rather than as a parent who never did enough.

Other episodes in my life - the sexual abuse and rape - were also re-lived as I wrote. At these times I became irritable, tearful, and horrible to live with. Once I had written these things down, lived through them again, and tried to understand and forgive the hurt they'd caused, they too retreated. Forgiveness came for all sorts of slights, and grudges I'd carried for thirty or more years were released and forgotten. I felt I'd shed kilos of emotional baggage, and was able to feel more relaxed.

The writing was healing, and became a kind of therapy for me. I had no intention of publishing it, but as the story unfolded I shared it with friends. They all felt it was a remarkable saga, and that it might help others who read it as well.

Now, three years since I wrote those first words I have a better idea of just who I am. From the cards, letters, phonecalls and emails I've received from all over New Zealand, the book helped many other people to figure themselves out too. This has been deeply rewarding, making all the long nights, rewrites, tears and fears worthwhile.

Bent Not Broken was a painful book to write. It has caused upset in my family; mostly among those who haven't read it. I feel though, from the overwhelmingly positive public reaction to it, that the book was well worth publishing.

The decision to bring out the book in two parts was a last-minute one. We ran into legal problems about some of the content of this latter part of the story, and had to either hold the whole book off, or publish in two parts. The last words of *Bent Not Broken* were "… but that's another story…"

Here is Part II, The Other Story.

Bent Not Broken
- a summary

A quick trip through my previous book,
for those who haven't read it,
or would like a refresher.

I am Lauren Kim Roche, a Scorpio baby, born in Wellington during the year of the Ox. I arrived on Guy Fawkes Day, 1961. Pam Roche, my mother, was eighteen when she had me. My father was twenty-one. They had been married for five months.

Two sisters followed; Tracey, born in 1963, and Shelley in 1965. Our parents fought. Dad was absent more often than not and Mum was stuck with three demanding kids under the age of four. When Dad found work in Whyalla, South Australia, we eventually flew over to join him.

Our parents had fights that were frightening yet exhilarating. Soon Mum's friendship with 'Stretch', a neighbour in the nearby caravan park, became more than just friendship. When Dad found out, Mum and Stretch took us and his family and left Whyalla in a convoy of cars and caravans. We had little money. During this time I was sexually abused by Stretch's father and brother, a horror that I kept to myself. When I returned to New Zealand to live with my grandparents, my life seemed to be changing for the better.

Life with my grandparents at Miramar was paradise. However, a few months later my mother and Stretch returned to New Zealand, and he got a job as a farm labourer in Featherston. Violence in their relationship meant this move was short-lived, and I soon returned to Miramar and my grandparents.

More changes were afoot. Stretch returned to Australia with his three children, and my father came back to Wellington. My mother moved in with my sisters, grandparents and me in Miramar, her room filled with music, incense and brass Buddhas. She became a drug abuser and she was drinking heavily, having rowdy parties when Grandma went away. Her depression worsened and she was committed to a psychiatric hospital.

In 1976, aged 14, I was holidaying in Auckland with my aunt, uncle and cousins. Rotoroa Island is hot, clean and idyllic; the holiday was full of walks and swims and hunts for shells. The phone rang early one morning. "Sit down, I've got bad news. Pam's dead." Mum was gone. My feelings about her were ambivalent but her death hit me hard. I suffered immeasurable guilt.

For two painful terms I went to Epsom Girls' Grammar in Auckland. I hated that school, but in spite of it all I made some friends. Together we formed a Bay City Rollers fan club, and went on weekend trips, one of which, to the Waikato River, yielded my first kiss.

I returned to Wellington where my Rollers fan club flourished. I began working, and experimented with eating disorders. Bored, and having met some Yankee sailors from the *Polar Star*, a visiting icebreaker, I made an impetuous decision. The ship was leaving for Seattle and so was I - as a stowaway.

The trip was three weeks of dark, cramped, smelly hell. When Joe, one of the sailors who had befriended me, helped me ashore I had shrunk several sizes. My hair was greasy and my lips cracked and bloodied where I had chewed the skin from them. After a shower and change of clothes I felt much better. I had made it.

Joe and I travelled to Oregon to visit his parents, and from there I went on alone to San Francisco to stay with my uncle Dave. I made a few friends and attended high school as a visitor for two days. I started to hang out with a bunch of boys, but again I decided to move on, planning to hitchhike to Long Beach via the West Coast. The world seemed grand, and I felt ten feet tall and bulletproof. I took a ride with three men and soon realised I had made a mistake. At an isolated beach, over several awful hours, they raped me. I had never been so frightened in my life. The next day I hitchhiked into Los Angeles, with wadded up socks in my knickers to soak up the blood from my wounds.

In Flagstaff, Arizona, I caught up with Willard from the Doctor Hook band; I had met him on their New Zealand tour. I continued hitching around the midwest, although now I carried a hunting knife concealed under a long sweatshirt. In Dallas Doctor Hook were performing. Between concerts I stayed backstage talking to the band.

So much had happened to me in such a short time. The excitement couldn't last and my spirits began to wane. My links with home were cut; I felt alone and far from help. So much for my new invincibility.

While weeping in a coffee shop I was befriended by a man who took me home and introduced me to his friends. They contacted the Immigration and Naturalisation Service, who in turn contacted the FBI. Two agents arrived to interview me. I was taken to a juvenile detention centre ('Juvie') where, among other things, we had art therapy. I knew how these games worked. I drew a big thundercloud all grey and black covering the whole page.

The immigration guys read my diary and interviewed the captain of the *Polar Star*. My story was checked and they confirmed my semi-secret presence on board. By this stage I wanted my Mum - too late, she had died - and I wanted to go home. The media had been alerted about the teenage stowaway in Texas and there was a buzz of interest in the story from America and New Zealand. Meanwhile the authorities transferred me to Dallas County Jail. I didn't want to leave Juvie, but the issue was settled.

After three weeks in prison I was on my way home, to

Miramar and Grandma and Tracey. No one was waiting at the airport. I got a ride with a radio journalist who did her best not to smirk at the painful accent I had picked up in my four months away.

I couldn't go back to school and I wasn't trained for anything. I got a job at McDonalds and was introduced to Pinkies, a popular prescription drug of the time, by my manager, Wayne. I became pregnant to Wayne, and although I fully supported a woman's right to have a pregnancy terminated, I did not want to go through with the procedure myself. Wayne ditched me.

At the Hole in the Wall club I found work as a stripper, doing a fire eating act. Performed in a G-string, the act took six minutes. During the day I was also spending time in the red light district. When my pregnancy became obvious I left the club and worked as a prostitute on the corner of Cuba and Vivian Streets, primarily targeting Japanese and Korean sailors. I worked the street until the fifth month of my pregnancy.

A hitchhiking tour of New Zealand followed. I visited Cape Reinga, Whangarei, Rotorua, Napier, and other beautiful places. I was picky about which cars I got into; I had learnt something at least from my American experience. Wherever I travelled I could not escape the reality that I was seventeen, pregnant and alone. No matter how long or far my journey, those facts remained unchanged. Eventually I had to return home.

My son Christopher was born in Wellington in 1979. We stayed in hospital for a week and bonded closely. After we left I started work at Kentucky Fried Chicken in Wellington. Soon my shifts lengthened, and two days a week became five. Grandma came to seem more like Christopher's mother than I did. Wanting the best for my baby, I vowed to become a full-time mother again and stopped working at KFC. I moved into a flat with my sister Tracey and her friend Jenny.

Tracey, Jenny and I had the usual adolescent weight hang-ups and started a different diet every couple of weeks.

Although we were never satisfied with the way we looked, we realised we had power over the men we met. We befriended some American sailors and I fell in love with Floyd, who had a broad smile and sexy muscles. My dream of returning to the United States was rekindled, and I needed cash. I became a masseuse at the San Francisco Bathhouse.

The girls at the San Fran took home 30 percent of what we earned from our massages. We were to be discreet about 'extras' and could keep all the money we earned from performing them. I decided I wouldn't do extras. Floyd wasn't thrilled about my new job but knew I had to do something to pay the rent and phone bill.

While I was at work Tracey looked after Chris. Though I was unaware of it at the time, my relationship with my son was slipping. One day I calculated how much more money I would be making if I did a few extras. The next day on my way to work I stopped and bought sexy new underwear and two dozen condoms. I was set for my new role.

Prostitution has been glamorised as a profession. Much of the time I worked in the parlour I felt I should have been trained in psychology, because so many of the men needed talk as much as sex, if not more. I began to drink two or three bottles of cheap bubbly a night, and I took pills bought from the other girls. It was a slow entrapment which I barely noticed happening.

Chris was growing up fast. I relied on Tracey, Jenny and Grandma to take care of him at night and while I slept during the day. It seemed the right thing to do at the time - exhausted from long and irregular hours of work, I was developing a short fuse and becoming increasingly despondent. I was turning into my mother but didn't realise it.

My fantasy remained, that escape to America would improve my life. All I needed was the cash and a visa. In the hope of gaining easy access to the States I married James Gee, a Canadian looking for a Kiwi visa. We stayed together for 36 hours.

Although I was miserable I still enjoyed some wild parties. On one memorable occasion I met Gina, a butch lesbian who introduced me to Sapphic sex. Regardless of such awakenings, I began to have my first major encounter with depression, starting with the erosion of my self-esteem and loss of motivation. It was during this time that I began to date Paul, a drug squad cop. As my relationship with Paul escalated I wrote to Floyd and broke off our long-distance dream.

Around this time the Springbok tour invaded New Zealand. I was involved in protests and earned myself my only police conviction during one. I paraded around the San Francisco Bathhouse wearing a 'Stop the Tour' badge. The management insisted I remove it; I refused. After midnight I was dismissed. I was free.

Having seen a GP about my depression, I was taking the anti-depressant Tryptanol. One bleak morning I took 143 of these pills in a suicide attempt which saw me admitted to a psychiatric unit for a month. By the time I was discharged I had made an important decision: to return to school as an adult student - I was twenty-one.

Although I loved being back at school, the hours of study and work meant I was seeing little of my son Chris. My relationship with Paul, which was at times exhilarating, contained destructive elements. He was possessive and demanding. When I realised I was pregnant to him it was not a cause for celebration. I decided to continue the pregnancy, alone, because Paul fled. My university plans would have to go on hold briefly, but I would not abandon them.

I got a flat near Grandma's, and Chris lived there with me. I finished the year with an A bursary. In the final fortnight of my pregnancy Paul appeared on the scene again. Chris, upset by the prospect of a baby in the house, began spending more and more time at Grandma's. Paul James Roche was born in May 1985. When he was eight months old I started the medical intermediate course at university.

Things were difficult. Not only was the course gruelling

but my partner Paul's mental health was deteriorating. Our son Paulie was diagnosed with an intellectual disability, hard to believe of this beautiful, laughing baby. Meanwhile I sat my exams and passed them all. Confident of getting into Medical School, I made plans to shift to Dunedin and was crushed to find out I had missed selection.

Paulie and I moved to Dunedin anyway, as I planned to do a Bachelor of Science. We had been there two weeks when a letter arrived - I had been accepted into Medical School after all. The training began, and my problems were compounded by my relationship with Paul, who had stayed in Wellington but kept trying to control me. He was unpredictable and his behaviour worried me. Retired from the police on psychological grounds, he was scary one minute, loving the next. He did, however, help me negotiate to buy a little house in Dunedin, my very own piece of the Kiwi dream.

After a series of suicide threats from Paul, I broke the relationship off. This left me free to track down Petal, a gay friend from the San Francisco days, who had contracted Aids. Taking a week off class I went to Auckland to be with my old friend. His long wait for death was wearing him down. Back in Wellington when Petal died, I was unable to go to the funeral, but I will always be grateful that I got to say goodbye. Another friend from the past, Maree, died not long after. I vowed to stop being ashamed of my past.

My relationship with Chris was improving, and Paul was spending time with Paulie and me in a non-threatening way. After a brief fling with a medical student, Clayton, I met another man, Bernard, a tall British boy who became my flatmate and lover. Although problems continued to plague me, I sat my final exams in late October, and passed. I had made it!

After I became a doctor, life continued to be challenging and less serene than I'd hoped...

Prologue

7 July 1999

L ynne, the receptionist at the medical centre where I worked, ran laughing into the tearoom.

"You'll never guess what the headline is. You'll die!" She was carrying a few copies of the weekly newspaper Contact. I reached for one, but she held it away, laughing.

"Come on Lynne, let me see it. Please."

The week before I'd been interviewed by a *Contact* reporter who'd heard from a friend that I was writing my autobiography. We sat together at Green House Books and talked for half an hour over coffee, and then he photographed me on the beach at Paraparaumu. I envisaged a modest article tucked away in the middle of the paper, not the monstrosity Lynne now handed me.

My story was on the front page. The headline, huge and black read: 'Stripper, Prostitute, Doctor'.

"Oh my God!" I squealed. My first thought was for my patients; what would they think about this? True, I wanted to publish the story of my life, but had always thought it would be low-key. No such luck.

The surgery phone rang. The nurses, receptionist and I looked at one another, before Lynne answered the call. A woman patient in her sixties wanted to speak to me.

"Lauren, I always knew there was something special about you. Good on you, dear."

A dozen people called that day with messages of support. Although it wouldn't be in the shops for another four months, people began ordering the book.

The story was out.

There was no going back.

1

I finished Medical School in November 1991. Only ten years earlier I had been working as a prostitute in the San Francisco Bathhouse in central Wellington.

My first job as a real doctor was on the geriatric wards at Wellington Hospital. There were two wards for the old people: Ward 5, which was dark and run-down, and smelled of urine and disinfectant. Medically ill elderly stayed there. Despite the efforts of the nurses, it felt like a dead-end place. I always hoped I'd never end up anywhere like it. Ward 2 was new and bright, and was the rehabilitation ward, for those who had 'graduated' from Ward 5, and were almost well enough to return home. It had a far more optimistic feel to it; partly due to the relative newness of the ward, and partly to the fact that the patients here were more likely to walk about the ward unaided or with sticks. Nurses usually wheeled those in Ward 5 about, if they were unable to use Zimmer frames.

Each medical placement lasts three months, during which time junior doctors are expected to learn all about the field they are working in. I loved 'Gerries'. The old people often had fascinating histories and were so grateful for any little assistance given them. An 80-year-old woman cried after I'd syringed years of wax from her ears; she could hear again. She'd spent so long unable to hear that she'd gradually lost her independence - now she hoped she'd be able to speak on the telephone again. Full of gratitude, she brought a tea set to the ward for me the next time she was admitted. I couldn't persuade her to keep it. I still have it, a reminder that doing the smallest of things for other people can have astounding results for them.

The speciality had its difficulties though. Often the people we cared for here had defective hearing and vision; others were confused and disoriented. On my first day on the job, I woke an ancient blind woman in Ward 5 to take her blood. Shaking her shoulder gently, I asked her if she was Mrs Green.

"Yes, Love, that's me."

"Sorry to wake you, Mrs Green, but I need to do a blood test on you."

"Oh, dear, you'll have such a trouble getting blood out of me. All right then." My patient sat up, pulling the sleeve of her bedjacket to expose the crook of her elbow. It was bruised from an earlier blood test. The other arm looked worse. Mrs Green trembled as I tightened the tourniquet around her arm. Her veins were thin-walled, and difficult to spear with the needle. When I tried to withdraw blood from them, the veins collapsed, as they often do in thin older people. After three attempts to take her blood, I gave up. Both Mrs Green and I agreed that was the best option. I went looking for my registrar, the more senior doctor on the ward.

"I'm trying to bleed Mrs Green, but having no luck. Will you please give me a hand?" My registrar raised his eyebrows before agreeing to help. We gathered together the equipment we'd need and entered Mrs Green's four-bed cubicle. The senior doctor walked up to the bed opposite the one I'd just left.

The real Mrs Green eyed us suspiciously before holding her arm out to be bled. I'd been trying to take blood from the wrong woman.

After that little lesson, I always read the name on a patient's identification bracelet before attempting any procedure on them. If someone was confused, or hearing-impaired, they might agree to anything, and it was my responsibility to make sure I was treating the right person. I was glad to have that lesson so early in my career.

My youngest son Paulie was now five and attending a school with a special needs unit. His intellectual disability was becoming more apparent as he grew. Paulie had blond curls and wore glasses that usually bore traces of all the major food groups. He was sturdy, quick and extremely strong. Paulie could turn on taps that other people needed a tool kit for. We lived in a flat on Mein Street, across the road from the hospital and next door to the hospice. The empty Hospital Board house next door had a small-calibre water pipe running from the upper storey to the ground. One morning Paulie got out of bed before me, unlocked our front door and wandered to the section next door. I was woken by his gleeful shouts. He'd bent next-door's water pipe back and forth until it ruptured. Water fountained from the broken pipe, making muddy puddles and streams at his feet. He splashed and danced and yelled, soaked to the skin, delighted with his work.

Paulie was fixated with water. Another morning he took off down the street, entered an occupied house, put the plug in the kitchen sink and turned the taps on full. When she found him, the woman who lived there chased him home. I understood her anger but simply couldn't restrain my son. He could undo locks and move unbelievably quickly once free. It's impossible for anyone who hasn't lived with one of these miniature escape artists to understand how difficult it is to contain them without tying them up; and no one would want to do that.

Sometimes I took both my sons to the hospital cafeteria for tea. Christopher - then eleven - lived with my grandmother. She had cared for him when I studied medicine in Dunedin, and he had chosen to stay on with her when I returned to Wellington. He spent some weekends with me. Chris was tall and blond and looked remarkably like his totally-absent father. He was handsome and articulate and I felt very proud of him. Chris had a way with people that made them trust and open up to him. I longed for him to live with me - I wanted my family complete again.

One day at the hospital caff I had to use the loo, and left the boys to their dinner. In the couple of minutes of my absence, Paulie disappeared. The hospital caff was on the eighth floor of a big block - there were four elevators and thirteen other floors where he could be. Chris thought Paulie was going to find me so had let him go. Half an hour later we found him on a ward, talking to a 'poor sick old person' - a twenty-five year old man recovering from surgery.

That same month, although only five, he was suspended from school for a week. His teachers had reached the end of their patience with him. He took off from school regularly, covering several kilometres and crossing major roads before being found. Each time he disappeared I'd be paged at work and would need to leave my ward to help find him. The police and taxi companies knew him well by this stage, so they too would watch out for him. If a special school couldn't contain my little boy, who could?

Paulie's dad Paul, my new partner Bernard and I talked long and hard about Paulie and his future. Paul had retired from the police force, and wasn't working, so he could spend more time caring for and protecting our son than I could.

Paul was well again, having beaten a severe depressive episode. He was going to university and looking at the world with hope and confidence. He had fully recovered and was back to being the caring person I'd fallen in love with years earlier. In many ways he was healthier than me. I was stressed, tired, and all too often close to tears. Despite loving my job, depression was closing in. I needed a break.

Paul lived on a ten-acre section, and could have animals, bikes, and other things that were impractical where I lived. I was on a busy street, not a safe place for a child with an intellectual disability and a fondness for running across roads. The decision to relinquish Paulie's care to Paul was the best one for all of us, but I was still wrecked the day he took Paulie to live with him. I tried to hide my tears from Paulie as I hugged him goodbye, but couldn't hold them back. He looked confused as he kissed me. Bernard held me in the front garden of our flat as I watched down the road after the departing car. My kids had both gone. Had the sacrifices I'd made to be a doctor been worth it?

In every other way I thought they had.

2

Bernard's parents phoned him from London every fortnight, and on one of the calls made an extraordinary offer. They wanted to pay for him, my children and me to visit them in England for Christmas. After hearing their offer I wandered around the flat in a daze. I was going to London! It was hard to believe his family's generosity. No one had given me such a gift before. I thought I'd take Chris, if he wanted to come, but not Paulie. Because of his wandering he would be a nightmare to travel with.

I saved my money, as I'd need plenty in the coming weeks. We'd need spending money for the trip to the UK, and there was also the formal graduation and capping ceremony coming up in Dunedin just before we went away. I was so looking forward to that. A real graduation, from Medical School - it still seemed unreal. I desperately wanted to attend. It would be the culmination of all the work I had done.

The image of myself in gown and mortarboard, shaking hands with the Dean and receiving my degree, had sustained me through the difficult parts of Med School. The low patches when I was trying to cope with Paul's vicissitudes as well as my own depression, and the times when there just wasn't enough money or hours in the day. There had already been a local graduation ceremony in Wellington, where I'd worn a backless red dress and showed off my tattooed back to the assembled parents and dignitaries. The real occasion was only a few weeks away, and would truly be my vindication.

Bernard and I got a new flat. As I was no longer a medical student I was ineligible for the one we were renting, and anyway we could afford something more salubrious now. Chris phoned one day from Grandma's to say that he'd like to come and live with us. I was too excited about this news to think deeply about why he had changed his mind. I'm still not sure why he did. Perhaps living with a doctor would mean he'd get better toys - like all his mates, he craved radio-controlled cars, fancy bikes and clothes, and the latest Walkman. Now he didn't have Paulie to compete with for my attention. Whatever the reason for his change of heart, I was thrilled that soon Chris would be a close part of our family.

My two boys were markedly different, but got on well together. Chris was bright and active, but always patient with Paulie and his obsessions. I believed, though, that he resented Paulie's status as the child who'd accompanied me to Med School. He was jealous of Paulie's close relationship with his father, too. Chris longed for some time with his own dad, who'd been absent from our lives since before he was born. Unknown to Chris, I'd been trying to track his father down so he could have some contact with him. I hadn't told him this, because I didn't want him to be too disappointed if I failed to locate him.

Bernard and I rented a house in Adelaide Road, Newtown, and enrolled Chris at Wellington South Intermediate School. We agreed he should have frequent contact with Grandma in Miramar, and would spend most weekends at her house. Grandma had been his consistent caregiver since he was born, and it would be unfair to both to suddenly part them.

Chris seemed settled with us. He was helpful and happy. He saw Grandma regularly, often walking from Newtown to her house, about an hour away on foot. It was wonderful to have my big boy back with me. I loved Chris intensely and felt I might be able to make up to him for the time I'd been absent from his life. I did all I could to rebuild the bond we'd once had.

The future was looking exciting. I worked eighty hours a week and spent little, as I wanted money to spend in London, and before that, in Dunedin at the graduation ceremony. I looked forward to seeing all my old classmates again and comparing horror stories about our first months on the wards. I wasn't reading my bank statements, as this might tempt me to spend the savings I needed for the near future.

One lunchtime I took leave from my ward and went into town to buy air tickets to Dunedin for graduation. Bernard wasn't coming to the ceremony; we thought the money for his fares would be better spent during our overseas holiday. I searched for my autobank card. It wasn't in its usual place in my wallet - perhaps I'd left it beside my bed - so I queued at the bank to withdraw the cash for my tickets. The teller shook her head as she passed me the piece of paper with my account details on it. My bank account, which should have held nearly two thousand dollars, was a thousand in overdraft.

The bank wouldn't let me withdraw any money for my airfares. There had to be a mistake.

I requested a detailed printout, and saw that five hundred dollars a day had been withdrawn from automatic teller machines over the past three days. My missing autobank card! Both Bernard and Chris knew my PIN number - I'd given it to Chris one day when Paulie was sick, and he needed ten dollars for a school trip. Oh God. I felt sick. Perhaps, though, Bernard had put the money into an interest-bearing account, just to surprise me, but I couldn't imagine why he'd do it in $500 increments. I tried, unsuccessfully, to put my panic on hold.

I phoned the manager of my local bank, who told me there'd been a further $500 withdrawal that day, as well as several other small purchases. He admitted the bank had erred in allowing my account to go so far over its limit, but reminded me I'd made the bigger error. Since I'd divulged my

PIN to someone else, I lost any right of appeal to the bank. I'd have to find the money and repay every single cent. He cancelled the autobank card at my request, and said he'd speak to the culprit for me, if I brought him in. Looking over my other accounts, he told me that Bernard hadn't transferred the money anywhere else. My last hope for the missing funds was gone.

It was a relief to have a bus concession ticket in my wallet. Without it I'd have been stranded in town. I couldn't concentrate when I got back to work - I felt so betrayed. Chris had stolen small amounts of money before, both from Grandma and me, but I imagined a great many kids were opportunistic petty thieves. I'd certainly nicked small amounts of money as a child if I saw them lying around. This was on a different scale altogether. It seemed that Chris's new-found helpfulness was not such a desirable thing after all. He was acting from a guilty conscience. I could have throttled him.

The nurses on my ward were sympathetic when I told them what had happened, but I felt so stupid. I had trusted a twelve-year-old with my PIN number, exposing him to a temptation he wasn't mature enough to resist. I was culpable, but still intensely angry. My emotions alternated between rage and guilt. I did the adult thing and settled for anger - I'd make him sorry.

I was first home that night. Bernard had a job managing the laundry at a private hospital, and Chris had an after-school activity. The two of them walked up the street together, having met on their way home. I was watching them through the net curtains in the lounge. Chris was carrying a big, new, remote-controlled car under his arm. It felt as though I was exploding with rage. I met them at the door. Chris smiled at me, and held the toy out to me.

"Look what my friend loaned me, Mum." I didn't let him say anything else, but flew at him. I remember kicking him in the shins and screaming at him to go straight to his bedroom.

Bernard stood with his mouth open, astounded. Chris

looked shocked. It seemed he really thought I'd never find him out.

The phone rang before I could explain my actions to Bernard. It was Chris's schoolteacher - did I know he was using my money card? He'd been handing out cash at school and buying toys for his new friends. I hung up and stormed into Chris's bedroom. He was lying on his bed, hugging his new toy to him. He denied any knowledge of the missing money. Why didn't I trust him? The teacher had it wrong. Why was I always picking on him?

Bernard tried to console me. He'd picked up the gist of what was going on from my words with Chris. I was crying, both from fury and grief. It was clear I couldn't go to graduation. Could we even afford to go to the UK? True, his parents were paying the airfares, but could we go with no money? There was no question now of Chris coming with us - it was him, or me.

I wanted to belt him. Anger greater than any I'd ever felt burned in me. I didn't hit him again - after the initial kick, I was afraid I wouldn't be able to stop. Hell, my Mum had once tried to kill me for less, and I didn't want to lose control the way she had. I vented my anger verbally instead. He'd have to pay me back - he'd better start looking for an after-school job now. I was on his case incessantly about the money: the disappointment and frustration of being unable to attend my graduation ceremony was overwhelming.

Next day I reported his theft to police Youth Aid workers, who took Chris from school and gave him a tour of the police cells in an attempt to steer him away from crime. They were surprised at the extent of the theft, and hoped a fright might discourage further offending. One of the policemen, quite intuitively I thought, asked if Chris was having sexual orientation problems, as this level of offending in young boys sometimes heralded such difficulties.

The police recovered $50 of the missing $2500. I confiscated anything Chris had bought with the money and sold it second-hand. He'd hidden some stuff under the house; the rest had been given to friends to hide. He didn't argue when I told him he was not coming away overseas with us for Christmas. The eternally tolerant Grandma said she'd have him, and that seemed enough for Chris.

Bernard's parents thought we were harsh, leaving him behind, but I just couldn't take him. I'd missed my graduation - one of the cruellest blows he could have struck - and I did not want him to have any kind of reward after his actions.

3

Three days before Bernard and I were to leave for London I had a phone call from a friend - George's former flamate. George was one of the gays I'd known at the San Francisco Bathhouse, and met again in Ward 26 at Wellington Hospital. He was now in Auckland hospital, dying from a brain infection, the consequence of Aids. He'd asked to see me. Bernard and I changed our flights, getting to Auckland a day earlier than planned, so I could say goodbye to my old friend.

George's wicked grin was almost all that was left of him. Like the Cheshire cat, it seemed all the other parts of him had dimmed or disappeared. He recognised me, and smiled, reaching his skeletal arms out for an embrace. Having learned from my experience when I visited the deathbed of Petal, another gay friend who had succumbed to Aids, I didn't squeeze George back, but gently stroked the bones of his spine through his skin. He reached up to wipe tears from my face, but missed my head entirely. The brain infection had destroyed his judgement of depth and distance. He asked me to help fill in his breakfast menu. George no longer had the co-ordination to use a pen - when he did get it under control in his hand he tried to write several centimetres away from the paper. He was close to death. I hugged and kissed my old friend, sad to leave him, but glad the indignity of his illness would soon be over. I thought about him constantly over the next week, wondering if he'd relinquished his grip on life. I learned later that he died the day after my visit.

At last we were off. Until the British Airways jet was heading down the runway, I really didn't think our trip would happen. I was going overseas, legitimately. My last big overseas trip had been a stowaway escapade on a Yankee icebreaker, aged sixteen. That trip had taken three weeks, which I'd spent curled in a ball in a dark compartment near the top of the ship. They didn't serve decent food and wine on the icebreaker, there wasn't even a loo to use. This was the way to travel! We were on a flight stopping only briefly in Perth and Japan. We didn't want to waste our holiday time with stopovers.

I felt nervous at the thought of meeting my lover's family. I was seven years older than him, and had children and 'a past.' Not that I was about to share the lurid details with them; I just wondered if they might see it written on my face. I hoped that my medical degree somehow negated all the minuses, and that they'd like me, approve of me as a mate for their son. My nerves got the better of me just out of London and I told Bernard I wanted to go home. He hugged me and reassured me that everything would be okay.

Bernard's parents met us at Heathrow and drove us to their classy home in Farnham, Surrey. Our flight had arrived at five in the morning. England seemed dark, busy, and cold. I was amazed at the miles upon miles of Coronation Street housing in London, and the extent of the green fields as we travelled south. How could a small country with so many millions of inhabitants still have room for fields and forests? I had always thought that Emmerdale farm on the telly was a tiny isolated pocket of green. Bernard insisted that his dad drive us down the main street of Farnham so I could see the Christmas lights. It was the first time I would spend Christmas in a cold climate and the darkened streets festooned with coloured lights looked magical, not incongruous as they do in the Antipodean brightness and heat.

Bernard's family home was set in a spacious garden with dignified trees and a venerable orchard. His mother had set up his old bedroom for us, pushing the two single beds together. We slept for hours, trying to chase off our jet lag. I woke several times, never quite believing I was on the other side of the world to my children. I wondered how Paulie was but tried not to think of Chris - the disappointment at missing my graduation was still sharp enough to bring me to tears.

Bernard's family were generous - they were welcoming, genteel and accepting of Bernard's choice of mate - even though I was an older woman, a colonial, and had a kid who was a criminal in the making. I loved them immediately. His parents were both quite reserved, and didn't seem to know how to react to me when I spent most of Christmas day in tears. Actually, due to the stress of the time and the environment we were in Bernard had hit me - an uncharacteristic act. Trying to protect him, I told them I was crying because I missed Paulie.

We spent three weeks in Farnham. Bernard spent days in bed, reading, ("I'm at home now, so I can do what I like"), so I went to London on the train with his younger sister Vicky, and visited most of the places I'd only ever seen on the Monopoly board - Trafalgar Square, Regent Street, Park Lane, Piccadilly. Having thought that Auckland was a big city, I was amazed at the vastness of London. We visited the London Dungeon and I read a plaque on the wall that said several Victorian prostitutes were buried in a grave now covered by the footpath outside. I wanted to buy flowers and lay them on the pavement for the unnamed working girls, but knew I could never explain to Vicky why I'd done such a thing.

Bernard's parents took us south one day. We visited the breathtakingly impressive cathedral at Winchester, where the remains of Jane Austen slumbered under the floor. There was a sense of history that I never felt in New Zealand - our country is so relatively young. Here it felt like I was soaking in thousands of years of tradition. I lit a candle for George, wondering how he was. I hoped he'd died and found a new peace. My fondest memory of him was of sitting beside the swimming pool at the San Francisco Bathhouse, while he sucked my toes. Perhaps he had an angel's toes in his mouth these days…

I telephoned both Paulie and Chris; they'd enjoyed their Christmas. Chris didn't seem resentful that he'd spent his time in Miramar rather than the UK.

Soon we were headed home. Bernard proposed to me in a coffee bar at Heathrow, in time to tell his parents when I accepted. I sensed his Mum was less than thrilled, but she was upset at farewelling her son again so I guessed I could forgive her. The airline had mucked up our tickets, so we travelled home in different rows. Newly engaged and separated already. I didn't think of it as an omen.

Wellington seemed so small, clean and bright compared with England. It was a relief to be home. I had a shower, changed my clothes and went directly to the Gerries ward. I had a big debt to pay, courtesy of Chris, so had to work every available hour. A couple of hours later I fell asleep in the ward meeting and was sent home by my registrar. Bernard arranged to pick Chris up from Grandma's that afternoon, so we could be a family again. I still felt resentful towards my son but knew I had to see him again and sort things out.

The word soon went out among the junior doctors that I was looking for extra work and my pager went off at all hours as my former classmates tried to off-load their call days. A normal hospital working day was eight hours long - the call days started at eight in the morning and finished between ten and twelve at night, depending on the workload and the grace of the overnight doctor. The usual roster arrangement meant working one call day in five or six. I picked up so much extra work; I was doing three to five call days in a week, as well as my usual duties. As my call nights were in Hutt, Wellington and Kenepuru Hospitals, the management paid for me to taxi to outlying shifts. A typical day would see me work at Wellington from 8 to 4, then catch a taxi to Hutt Hospital where I would work till 10 or 11, then taxi home.

I was working as a rugby doctor, too, stitching up Bernard's Wellington College Old Boys team mates on the field, and reducing dislocated shoulders and kneecaps for them. Although this didn't pay much at all, I loved the challenge.

On one of my first games as team doctor, one of the players injured his shoulder. I was working that day with a female physiotherapist, and we ran onto the field to attend to the injured man lying in obvious pain on the ground.

"My shoulder, I've bloody hurt my shoulder." he groaned and writhed.

"Let's get you off the field and have a look. Can you walk okay?" I asked.

"Get me a doctor."

"I am a doctor, Dave. Let's get you up."

"But I want a REAL doctor." He looked serious.

The physiotherapist and I helped him from the field and examined his shoulder. In the changing room later I told him he was lucky to have got away with only one injury. I'd been tempted to give him a groin one as well. He laughed, happy with the treatment he'd received, and assured me he'd been joking. I never had another problem with the team after that.

Bernard was happy with all my work - the money coming in was bounteous. Chris didn't mind - if I wasn't at home, I couldn't hassle him about the money he had stolen. Bernard let him stay up later at night than I did, too. I got over my fear of medical emergencies by immersing myself in them, and also continued to 'prove my worth' to anyone who was watching. All told, my long hours worked well for everyone at our house.

4

D r Hook, the band I'd been associated with during my stowaway episode, was back in New Zealand for a series of concerts. A journalist from the Evening Post, having heard I was now a doctor, asked me if he could do a story about me. He wanted to call it 'Doctor, I Like Your Medicine', and run a photo of me with the band. I asked him not to, afraid that if any of my colleagues or patients knew that I'd been a 'teenaged blue-eyed groupie' they wouldn't take me seriously as a health professional. The journalist replied that the story of my stowing away was a matter of public record, and he could rehash it without my permission. Agitated, I phoned the paper's editor, and begged him not to run the story. They didn't, much to my relief. The incident still frightened me, though. The press had long memories. What other bits of information about my past did they have?

Bernard enjoyed the challenge of running the private hospital laundry, and it was refreshing to have two incomes again. He was selected for the New Zealand Universities rugby team, which was about to defend the Students' World Cup in Italy. We were both rapt about his selection. He was a lock, and a talented, if patchy, player. About the time of this selection, he was awarded a University Blue for rugby.

The week before the university team was to leave for the World Cup I had an early phone call at work from the police. A burglar had been caught in our flat, and they wanted me to return home to identify items they'd found in his possession. My upstairs neighbour had heard someone knocking on my front door, and then smashing a window to enter the house. He called the police on seeing the burglar climbing through the broken window. When I arrived home, the cop on the scene told me that he believed the offender's motive had not been solely burglary. The man found in my house had a history of violent sexual offending, and had been imprisoned for the rape and battery of a local female taxi driver. He had ridden in her cab, raped and beaten her, then locked her in the boot of her car, leaving her to die on an isolated coastal road. Her injuries were so extensive that friends and family had been unable to identify her when she was found, fortunately still alive. This man told the police he'd been watching our house for several days, and knew when we left each morning. The morning he broke in, Bernard and I had an argument, and I left the house half an hour earlier than usual. Bernard left alone at our normal time. The cop said the burglar might have thought I was still in the house when he broke in.

The man pleaded guilty to breaking and entering and was fined; some of the money was given to us to replace the broken window. He came to see me as a patient about a month later, at the practice that I was locuming at. Recognising his name, I asked the nurse to tell him I was too busy to see him. I was too disgusted to look him in the eye, knowing what he'd done to another woman.

The fortnight that Bernard was in Italy, I slept poorly, worried that only Chris and I were in the house. In the weekend when he was at Grandma's house, I slept in Chris's room, as it felt more secure.

Things didn't improve with Chris. He got a job as a newspaper boy at Wellington Hospital, but I heard rumours that patients on the wards he covered were losing money. He was sacked before I could confront him about the thefts. He was short-tempered and nasty, and took to running away to Grandma's several times a week. He'd take off through his bedroom window if Bernard and I were awake; otherwise, we'd rise in the morning to find he'd gone. We tried to get Grandma to call us if he arrived at her house, so we could collect him, but she refused. Soon she began to lie about whether or not he had reached her place.

Grandma's whole life had been spent looking after other people. Chris was the latest in a string of family members she had cared for in her house in Miramar. It must have been lonely for her, living by herself in the house her father had built when she was ten. A house filled first with her father and five brothers, then as she'd grown up, her husband and eight children. After they'd all left home she looked after my Mum, then my sisters and me, and finally my son. Grandma loved and needed to look after other people. It was so hard for her to let go of Chris. She also felt safer with a young man in the house. Perhaps it was selfish of me to try and separate them.

From his behaviour, it seemed that his decision to live with Bernard and me had been the wrong one.

My cousin Jacquie, who lived in Featherston with her husband Steve and three kids, offered to have Chris for the school holidays. He was rapt about the invitation.

Jacquie had a soft spot for Chris who was delighted to be spending time with his 'Aunty'. He loved her dearly, and had lost contact since she'd moved away from Wellington when he was six. Chris almost floated off on his holiday. I warned Jacquie to keep her wallet and cigarettes well hidden, as he was a thief. This seemed a bit disloyal to him, but I needed to warn people if I allowed him to stay with them. Bernard and I were able to relax now we had the house to ourselves. It seemed Jacquie had done us all a huge favour, and we were grateful to her.

During his stay in Featherston, Chris spent a week at a Christian 'Live and Learn' camp. How prophetic the name of that camp turned out to be.

5

Chris returned from his three-week break even more secretive. Sure, he was entering his teens, but things seemed a little worse than they should. He showed Bernard and me a couple of photos he'd been given by the camp leader. Both showed three or four boys, Chris included, grouped around a middle-aged man. The camp leader was fat, grey-haired and ordinary, and was wearing a brown button-down cardigan and beige pants. He looked benign enough. Chris told us he was Terry - a worker for the St John's ambulance service, a bushmaster who took boys on treks for the Scouts, and a good guy. Terry was Chris's new best friend, and had invited him to spend the occasional weekend in the Wairarapa with him. They could go camping together, he told us, excitedly. Terry had a wife, but she was too sick to do anything, they even slept in separate beds, so she didn't mind him having visitors or special friends to stay.

This didn't sound right. Compounding my worries was the arrival of letters to Chris - every two to three days - and daily phone calls from Terry, which Chris insisted on taking in another room. I asked Chris if anything was wrong, and if anything had happened at camp. He flew at me in a rage, accusing me of calling his friend "a pervert". My explanations that it was unusual for a man in his fifties to keep such close contact with a twelve-year-old boy went unheard. Chris was furious. Fortunately, he was at school during the day, which gave me the chance to search his room. I didn't like invading his privacy, but it seemed to me that my boy was in some sort of trouble. There were no letters or photographs to find - Chris kept them on him at all times. I would have to intercept his mail as it arrived. I walked home each lunchtime to check the mailbox before Chris got home from school.

That day there was a letter and my heart lurched as I opened it. There was a telephone card in it, with instructions to call Terry from the phone box up the road, so I wouldn't know about it. Terry also elaborated on the offer to take Chris into the bush. They'd sleep in a pup tent, and zip their sleeping bags together to keep each other warm. This was okay - he said - he'd done it with lots of other boys before. He also gave Chris the phone number of a Scout leader in Wellington's eastern suburbs, and told Chris he should join this man's scout troop. Terry and the scoutmaster had several 'special friends' in common.

The letter was full of innuendo. There was no proof that Terry had abused Chris, but ample evidence that he was grooming him for some. I spoke to a counsellor at the Child and Family clinic, who felt, as I did, that there were not yet grounds for a police complaint, especially since Chris was so vehement in his denial of any wrongdoing.

I decided to replace the letter in the mailbox, having sealed it again, and read more of the letters from Terry as they arrived. I also told Chris, in response to his constant questioning, that I wanted to meet Terry before I'd let him stay with him. I didn't want to confront Terry, as I was afraid to drive their relationship further underground. If that happened there would be little chance of halting any further abuse - of my son or anyone else's.

After another week of letters - all of them ambiguous, but damning enough - I handed them to the counsellor, who forwarded them to the police. Chris was questioned, and angrily denied any wrong had been done. He was furious with me. Grandma told me I had a filthy mind for suspecting any dirty goings-on. Hell, Terry was a Christian! How could he hurt anyone?

6

Chris eventually seemed to forgive me for my suspicions about his 'friend' Terry. He received no more mail from him, and appeared resigned that I didn't want him to join the Scout troop Terry had recommended. He was making an effort to play by the rules, and was being genuinely helpful around the house. I tried not to feel suspicious about his change in behaviour.

I was on a three-month attachment to the emergency department at Wellington Hospital. The week before I started this job I watched the TV programme *Casualty*, hoping to pick up some tips. The thought of working in a speciality where anything could - and did - happen was exhilarating. The rugby doctoring had taught me a few emergency skills, and I was looking forward to using them in a proper clinical environment. The work was a combination of adrenaline-pumping emergency, run-of-the-mill medicine and tedium. Sometimes hours would pass with no patients, and it was hard to stay awake and enthusiastic for the next person needing our attention. The nurses were superb. I often thought they could manage without the junior doctors who intruded on their space. They were always available for advice and guidance, and were special people.

One of my patients was a young man who had been injured in a brawl. His girlfriend brought him into Cas, and stayed with him while I examined him. He had a dislocated shoulder and a few cuts and bruises. The shoulder had been out for about an hour, so severe muscle spasm meant it wouldn't be easy to pop back in without some strong pain-killers and muscle relaxants. I gave him an injection to loosen everything up and began to clean and stitch his cuts. He turned to his girlfriend who was angry with him for getting himself into this mess. "You know, Shirley," he said to her, his voice wobbly with drugs and emotion. "You're the most beautiful girl in the whole world, Shirley." His eyes went misty and he squeezed her hand.

"Please, Doc" whispered Shirley. "You've got to give me some of those drugs to take home. He's never said anything like that before." Her voice wobbled too. My heroic patient, now completely relaxed, began to snore. It was a true 'Mills and Boon' moment.

One Sunday afternoon when he was thirteen, Chris was overdue from an overnight visit to a friend's place. He was five hours later than he'd promised to be, and I was worried. I phoned Grandma's house, to find he wasn't there. Next I called the friend's house, and left a message on the answerphone. I sat down to await Chris's return. Bernard was doing something with his rugby team, and this was my first free weekend in ages. I tried to read a book and relax, but couldn't rid myself of the feeling that something was wrong.

A couple of hours later, the phone rang. It was the mother of the boy Chris had spent the previous night with. She didn't know where the boys were, but wondered if I'd heard from the police yet. Chris and his friend had stolen a car, and were missing in it. She asked me to call her back if the boys turned up at my house.

The next phone call, around nine at night, was from the police. Chris and his friend had been apprehended in a stolen car. Was I able to confirm for them that the man I lived with owned a .22 rifle? The boys had a gun and ammunition in their possession, and they claimed it all belonged to Bernard. The only person I knew of with guns was Paul. I rang him, and after searching his house he was able to confirm that his gun cabinet had been broken into, and a rifle and some boxes of ammunition were missing.

The police brought Chris back to my house an hour later in a squad car. Bernard pulled up outside the house in a friend's car, in time to see my son escorted to the front door. Before going to his room, I made Chris tell me what he'd been up to.

The night before he had decided to steal a gun and kill Bernard and me so he could live free from our interference. He and his twelve-year-old friend planned to tie up, beat, and then rob the friend's grandmother of her dead husband's gun. They would then come to my place, and ambush me when I got home from work.

They got to the old woman's house, thoroughly charmed her, and decided over tea and cake that they should find someone 'not so nice' to beat and rob. They stole her car instead, drove to Paul's house, and broke into it, stealing a rifle and over a hundred rounds of ammunition.

To my great good fortune, the grandmother notified the police her car was stolen, and the boys were pulled over by cops before they could do any damage.

Chris stared me out as he told his story, and I still don't know if he really intended to shoot me or not. I certainly believed that night he meant to.

When he'd finished explaining his actions, he stamped off to his room, climbed straight out the window and was off to Grandma's place. Bernard and I decided to let him go.

I pulled a chair over the front door that night, after double-checking that the house was locked up.

When, later that month, Jacquie and Steve asked if Chris could go to live with them, we grasped at the opportunity. Terry hadn't written to Chris again at our place, and Bernard and I believed there would be no further contact between them. Jacquie and Steve felt that immersion in a Christian environment might help Chris sort out his anger and stealing. I hoped a change of scene might achieve the same ends.

7

Paulie was thriving at Paul's house, and his new school, Petone Central. He had space to roam, farm animals to pet, and a school that could mostly contain him. The only major escape attempt came early in his time there, and was as impressive as his earlier efforts had been. He took off from school in the middle of the day, to be found by the police in mid-afternoon, wet from the chest down, and wearing shitty pants. He told them he'd tried to cross the Hutt River, but it was "too deep and too fast", so he'd climbed up the bank, and run across "the busy, busy road" until he reached Avalon Park - several kilometres from his school. Once again, I thanked his guardian angel. Someone was watching out for my six-year-old son.

I was still working a ridiculous number of hours on call, but loving the job and the challenge. The money was a bonus, but I still managed to spend more than I earned. Bernard and I had a full wine-rack, and bought new books and clothes most weeks.

When they are on a medical ward, junior doctors take turns at carrying the cardiac arrest pager. This was activated in any situation where someone's heart or breathing stopped, and they needed resuscitation. The pager had a different tone to the usual one - it was shrill and persistent, and continued bleeping for several minutes rather than a few seconds. Neither the doctor nor anyone else in the vicinity could mistake the urgency of the arrest page. Five of them were active at any time - the others being held by more senior doctors. The first year house surgeons were the most junior docs to be carrying one on each shift.

Like other duties, working the medical wards was hectic most times, boring at others. One night I was drinking coffee in Casualty during a quiet spell. My wards were in a different area of the hospital, but I'd been called down here to see someone, and had stayed on for a rest when I'd finished. The two pagers I was carrying (the routine ward pager and the cardiac arrest one) were silent, so I wandered down to the fracture clinic where there was a pile of books and magazines. I was too tired for a 'heavy' book, so looked for the lightest diversion I could find. There was a 'Sweet Valley High' paperback, and I picked it up. Hell, you couldn't get much more lightweight than an American teen romance. I checked that my pagers were turned on, put my feet up and began to read. I'd been into the story for about fifteen minutes when the cardiac arrest pager went off. Stuffing the book into the pocket of my white coat, I called the operator to see where the emergency was.

Someone in Coronary Care, at the other end of the hospital needed attention. I ran, taking the stairs to the main corridor two at a time. My stethoscope swung around my neck, and my tendon hammer dug into my leg as I ran. Junior doctors have a surprising arsenal of medical equipment in their coats: I think this is more for their own reassurance than that of their patients.

Hospital visitors and other doctors stood aside - the urgency of the bleeper unmistakable. Running along the main corridor I saw a lift about to close.

"Hold the lift," I called, racing towards it, "cardiac arrest!" The drama of the situation caused my voice to waver. The elevator was full of medical staff, patients and visitors to the hospital, who moved towards the back wall to make room for me. My white coat, its pockets full, hit my legs as I raced to my sick patient. It was like a scene from a medical drama - the young physician about to save a life … or so I thought, until the book I'd been reading in fracture clinic fell from my pocket - cover up, exposing my guilty secret.

I read *Sweet Valley High* books.

All of them could now see that I was just a little girl pretending to be a doctor. Thoroughly deflated, I entered the lift, red-cheeked from embarrassment rather than exertion.

When I got to the coronary care unit the emergency was over, and the nurses smiled at me: so much for medical dramas.

I loved being a rugby doctor - it appealed to my sense of the theatrical - listening to spectators gasp as I sutured the players on the sidelines was a real buzz. I now cared for the players in the Wellington 'B' squad, as well as Bernard's club side. Working with the 'B' team meant free travel around New Zealand when they played away games. I lost count of the number of times flight attendants told me how they envied my job! It certainly was fun to spend time in the changing room with fifteen or more superbly fit naked young men; however as I thought of the players as patients, all of them (except my boyfriend) were out of bounds for perving, so I perhaps didn't appreciate the perks of the job as much as a non-health-professional might have. On one trip to the upper North Island, we travelled by bus rather than plane. The trip up was quiet, as the players needed to be in shape for the next day's game. They relaxed, one played guitar while others sang. I tried to read a textbook, but quickly grew bored with that, so spent my time watching the countryside roll by. I had a great sense of belonging with the team, and never once regretted the time I spent with them, even though this ate into my sleep and rest times. The guys appreciated my services too. Having a team doctor who could sew up their cuts and treat infections and muscle strains meant they didn't have to queue in overcrowded accident and emergency clinics for care.

On this trip there were no major injuries, and everyone was fit for the after-match drinking session. After showers and the official function, we boarded the bus home. There were gallons of alcohol sneaked onto the bus, and the drinking continued - surreptitiously at first. The problem with drinking on a bus with no loo was soon apparent. The driver pulled over regularly, sometimes at public toilets, other times at roadside shrubs and trees. No one had thought of the poor doc - the only female on the bus. It is infinitely easier for men to pee outside than it is for women. I had to walk a few metres away from the standing men, find an appropriately large bush or tree to keep me out of their sight - as well as that of the passing traffic - and squat without wetting my shoes or trousers. The guys soon got sick of me taking longer than they did, and there were a couple of good-natured, though vociferous, complaints about the doc's peeing, especially from the non-drinkers in the team. At least I waited to get off the bus…

8

It was time to make a decision about my medical future. I wanted to specialise in Obstetrics and Gynaecology, and spend at least a couple of years doing advanced training in the UK. The main attraction with obstetrics and gynaecology was working with women and their pregnancies. I also felt I'd had a rough deal from the profession during my pregnancies, and felt that I might be able to make some woman-friendly changes from the other side of the sick-bed. Had my obstetrician listened to me and taken action over my concerns about my baby's lack of movement near the end of my pregnancy, would Paulie's disability have been avoided? Perhaps it would have made no difference at all, but I'll never know, neither will he, and we will always wonder.

Obstetrics and gynaecology encompasses both medical and surgical skills, and involves working with people who are mostly healthy. While still a med student I loved delivering babies and caring for pregnant women, and found this work very rewarding. I was already studying for my Part One examination in Obstetrics and Gynaecology - the first of the specialist exams in any chosen field. It is unusual to begin to study toward Part Ones without first working in that speciality area, but I thought things might be a bit easier this way. There was a hiatus in my stress levels; Bernard and I were alone, and who knew how long that might last.

To study for the exams I gave myself a solid six months, and took my textbooks everywhere with me while I worked. I studied at home, in hospital wards, and on the edge of rugby fields. I was utterly focused on my goal. It was the only way I could see myself making it.

I heard from Chris every couple of weeks. He was enjoying high school, and had joined the Air Cadets. He wanted to learn to fly one day. Things looked brighter for him than they had for a long time. Jacquie had caught him stealing a couple of times, and she and Steve had dealt with it inside the family unit. There seemed no need to worry too much about him.

Occasionally I saw Grandma. She'd never fully forgiven me for taking Chris away from her house, so things were icy between us. They were about to get worse.

There was no intimation that day that things would go horribly wrong. It was seven-thirty on a Saturday morning - my peaceful time of day, the hour before Bernard woke and the world began. I was in Chris's old room, which I'd turned into my workspace, and was studying the physiology of pregnancy, a subject that I loved, and excelled at. The next twenty-five minutes were so real; it is as if they are in the here and now - forever current - never finished.

The phone rings - unusually early for the weekend - I'm pissed off that someone is interrupting my solitude. It's my cousin Jacquie.

"How are you, Lon?" ('Loni' was always her pet name for me). She sounds stressed.

"OK, Jac. What's up?" She's alternately dragging on a cigarette and crying. My heart is in my mouth.

Jacquie begins to speak rapidly. "I didn't want to tell you - it's been going through my head for a week - but I've got to let you know."

"What? What's happened?" Someone has poured a bag of cement into my gut. It has to be about Chris. What has he done now? Stealing? Drugs? Expulsion from school? There seems to be enough time for me to imagine a hundred scenarios - all of them awful: none of them awful enough.

"I caught Chris with my daughter Melissa … in his bedroom. Umm, oh fuck, he was…"

Jacquie doesn't swear, I thought with part of my mind. My other thoughts are miles away. There's a scream echoing around in my head - bouncing from bone to bone in my skull. My legs don't want to hold me any more.

"…he was in between her legs. Her pants were off … he had his fingers inside her." She drags on her smoke and hiccups like a distressed child.

STOP!!!!!!!!! My mind cries out. NO MORE!!!!!!!!!

"Lon, she is only eight years old! He was abusing an eight-year-old girl."

Christopher, my son Christopher, has sexually abused a child. He is only thirteen - a child himself, but old enough to know better.

Jacquie regains her voice. I only half hear what she's saying. The cement in my guts has solidified. I'm stunned. I've walked through to the dining room. I look for somewhere to sit. No good - there's ironing and textbooks on all the chairs. I settle on the floor in front of the old gas fire. It's like the one in Grandma's house when I was a kid. I look at its broken heat conductors, and at the way the protective wires surrounding it have bent and burned, and at the discarded matches in the grate. I make a pile of the dead matches as Jacquie continues her tale.

Chris had been spending a lot of time with her children and the neighbour's kids, who came over to play most days. They'd been up in the playhouse, and in the bedroom - with the door closed. Jacquie had become worried. Not suspicious of course - who'd have imagined what would happen?

Chris was trouble; that was for sure. He'd been stealing and lying, but there'd been no sign that this sort of thing might happen. She hadn't told me how bad things had got, as she didn't want to worry me. The biggest problem was that Melissa, Jacquie's daughter, wouldn't talk about what happened. No one knew the extent of the abuse, and Steve and Jacquie didn't want her questioned or examined by police or social-workers in case this made things worse for her. One thing she did say. Chris had threatened her that if she told anyone about what had happened between the two of them, he'd cut her tongue out. She had to keep her mouth shut forever. No, Jacquie said, he hadn't actually *been* violent… Who knows what had really happened though, when the playhouse and bedroom doors were shut?

I feel Jacquie's pain. She is so full of self-recrimination. She wants to protect the neighbour's kids, her own children as well as my son, and, incongruously, me. She and Steve don't want the police involved, as they believe this will magnify their daughter's trauma. Chris is adamant he hasn't touched Jacquie's other kids, or any others, and on questioning her two sons, she believes they're fine. She can obviously no longer have Chris living in the same house as them though.

My cousin and I are devastated. We both have first-hand experience of the effects of abuse, and we'd hoped it would stop with our generation. Now my son has abused one of my cousin's children, under her roof.

I've heard enough. I have to go and get some air. I'll call Jacquie back. She won't let me go - not yet - Chris wants to speak to me.

I don't know what to say, or think, or do. I'm walking around the room now. I stop at the window. The Venetian blinds - once white, now a grubby cream - are half-open. As my eldest son comes to the phone, I run my finger over one of the metal fins of the blind. It comes away with a coating of soft dust - soft as the down on the cheek of the newborn I'd cradled almost thirteen years ago - the newborn turned monster. I must clean these blinds some day.

"Hi Mum." His voice sounds perky, his words clipped.

"Chris." Nothing more comes out. I'm painfully aware of a buzzing in my ears, a sense of light-headedness, unreality.

"Mum, I'm sorry." His voice is quiet, distant, yet I perceive a hint of excitement, of gloating even. I lose my detachment.

"It's a bit fucking late for sorry." I scream. "What the hell have you been doing?"

"I'm sorry, I said." He is petulant, whining now.

"Well you can't stay there. Jesus Christ, Christopher, you begged to live with them, now you treat them like this. How could you? They trusted you. Jacquie loves you. How could you?" I'm choking with anger. "What else did you do?"

"Nothing. It was the first time. There was nothing else."

I don't believe him.

"What about Jacquie's sons?"

"Of course I didn't touch them. It was just the girl, only once." He's sulky now, sulky and defensive. I want to hit him, make him react in some way other than this dead mono-tone. I despise smacking, and never hit him as a child. God, I thought it was a sort of violence leaving him to cry as a baby - he couldn't whimper for more than thirty seconds without attention, a cuddle, or a feed. I want to smash him. Did I create this monster?

"I can't speak to you. Get Jacquie for me."

Jacquie comes to the phone, taking a deep drag on her cigarette before speaking.

"Lon, I'm so sorry." I hear the tremor in her voice. She still wonders if telling me was the right thing to do. She needs no words to say this to me. My heart goes out to her.

"What have you done about it, Jac? Have you contacted the authorities? He needs some counselling - so does your daughter."

"We'll get the pastor to speak to them. We'll ask God to heal them both, that way the police don't need to know. It'd be horrible for her to have to relive it for the cops. You know that."

"But Chris needs help too. Normal 13-year-old boys don't do this sort of shit. If he's not stopped, there might be other kids."

"It's okay, Lon, we're handling it."

"We've gotta get him out of your place."

"Yeah, I know." She takes another long drag on the smoke.

"Listen, Lon. I gotta go. Talk to you later. Love you."

I hold the dead telephone receiver in one hand, striking the other palm with it - but the physical pain doesn't help me make sense of what has happened. Maybe there's no sense to be made. I drop the phone and wander through the house. It's just before eight in the morning. That call took only twenty-five minutes in real time, yet a lifetime in another sense.

My son is an abuser.

Everything has changed.

9

Bernard was asleep in bed. He liked to lie in on a Saturday morning, and relax before his rugby game, but I couldn't let him sleep. I couldn't handle this on my own.

I sat on the bed beside him, stroking his head till he woke. He listened to the horrible news and grew angry. Angry with Chris, with Jacquie and Steve and with the faith they place in the church. Bernard couldn't begin to understand my pain, or Jacquie's - the memories this threw up for us. I was eight, too, when I was abused, and Jacquie not much older. He was sympathetic and quiet, while shaking with rage and indignation. There was no way his sheltered Surrey upbringing had prepared him for this.

We went to the rugby. Bernard played well; I dealt with four injured players. The physiotherapist and coach wanted to know what was wrong with me. I was usually full of laughter and energy; that day it seemed I could barely drag myself around the field.

I told them what had upset me, but the continued repetition that my son was a child molester didn't make it feel any more real. The shock made me feel bruised inside and out, and as though I needed to strike my head to clear clouds out of it. I knew that people didn't really want to hear what I had to say, but I needed to tell someone.

On Monday, from my ward, I called a colleague who worked as a psychiatrist near Featherston, the town where

Chris was staying. I tried to organise counselling for him, but as I was not currently his guardian, and Jacquie wouldn't allow it, I had no luck. Besides, there was a waiting list for troubled adolescents, and he told me that the victims of abuse have a greater need than the abusers themselves. In fact, there was no established programme in the area for adolescent sex offenders.

The psychiatrist was sympathetic, but a lack of funding had left him unable to do anything for several weeks, if at all.

I rang the Children and Young Person's Service - CYPS. They provided counselling for the victims of sexual assault, but not the perpetrators. I argued that every untreated abuser has the potential to clock up many more victims. The social worker agreed, but again, said there was no funding for them to work in this area.

I considered calling the police, but Jacquie had begged me not to.

My standard of work was slipping - I could only concentrate on my quest for assistance for Chris. I thought there must be something that could be done to help him. There wasn't.

Jacquie called me again. Her husband's anger at Chris had grown to the point where she feared for his physical safety. It almost seemed that she was more worried about Chris than her own kids, but I knew that wasn't true. Jacquie was trying to forgive him, and her concern for his well-being was a reflection of that. Jacquie is one of the truest Christians I know. She and her husband decided to hand Chris's care to the Department of Social Welfare. I concurred with this decision - I thought if he returned to live with me at that point, I'd have killed him myself. Besides, I needed to keep my house safe for Paulie, who now spent most weekends and holidays with Bernard and me.

I told Grandma about Chris's offending, and she accused Melissa of being "a filthy little liar". She would not accept that Chris could do anything wrong, and sought to find a way to blame me, or Jacquie, if anything had happened. She told me I had a filthy mind for even considering he may be an abuser.

Given the way she was, there was no other way Grandma could have responded. It was stupid of me to think she'd ever think ill of 'her Chris'. I loved Grandma, but just wished she could see what was going on.

10

My exam preparation was going well, although my hospital work was suffering. I felt constantly exhausted, and was worried that I might make a bad decision with a patient. I found I was asking more senior doctors to double-check all my work. My constant worrying about my son - what was he doing, how was he coping, would I ever be able to get help for him - was wearing me down.

I arranged to take three months off to study, and fortunately this time came around before I made any mistakes. I had rediscovered the joy of learning, and the way a textbook could transport me away from the real world - not an attractive place at the time. I kept a journal, and wrote in it of hugging my texts to me, so excited by the possibilities and the knowledge they contained. I didn't write in my journal about the tears that were becoming more frequent, or about my plummeting self-esteem. I didn't want to recognise that depression, my black bear, was once again sneaking up on me. In the early stages of depression I always felt ashamed of my supposed weakness, and tried to hide the truth from myself, as well as other people.

My day was full of study. I'd rise about 6.30 or 7, and spend twelve to fourteen hours in my study reading about and memorising the location of the tiny nerves and blood vessels in the pelvis and abdomen. I learned the surgical landmarks in a woman's body so that when I was performing surgery I'd know what lay beneath my scalpel. I went to special anatomy and embryology lectures held at the School of Medicine for doctors studying towards Part One exams. It was an exciting time intellectually. Once again I was using my brain and my determination to take me towards another goal. If only my personal life was in order, I thought, things would be perfect.

The Part One exam was being held in London in September. I chose to sit the British exams as I intended to one day live there with Bernard and do further post-graduate training. There was an option of doing New Zealand exams, but the expense of the airfares was worth paying. I'd finally managed to repay the bank the money Chris had stolen a couple of years earlier, and had some spare cash at last.

In July, just before Chris's fourteenth birthday, I saw a psychiatrist. I could no longer deny to myself that I was falling apart. Despite my love for Bernard our relationship was suffering too. I didn't have enough energy to spare for him. My sleep was erratic, I felt afraid, tearful and tired, and the only joy in the whole world was to be found in my textbooks. I would be thirty-two in four months - the age at which my mother had committed suicide. I began to believe that I would die at that age also.

The doctor diagnosed a further bout of depression and prescribed Prozac, the new wonder drug. I hoped that I would soon feel normal again.

11

Bernard proposed to me again - this time on bended knee in the lounge. A Dave Dobbyn CD was playing - 'You Are A Joy To Live With'. It seemed so romantic.

We planned to wed early the following year, when his parents and older brother would be visiting New Zealand. My exam trip to the UK would be an opportunity for his family and me to get to know one another a bit better before the big day.

I travelled alone to London, and stayed with Bernard's family. I spent my time on the plane reading *Gray's Anatomy*, an impressive looking tome, and brushing up on the finer points of the female pelvis.

The exam was in the third week of my stay: I'd arranged my schedule so that I would become acclimatised and recover from jet lag before sitting the two papers. I revised my notes for ten to twelve hours every day, and loved this chance for uninterrupted study. Chris and his problems were several thousand miles away, and I didn't allow them to touch me. Bernard's brother John and his girlfriend Nicola lived in Notting Hill. As I studied at the desk they'd put in the lounge for me, I could hear young people playing in the street outside. A young West Indian man was chatting up some teenage girls one afternoon, telling them he was a gynaecologist, so just the man they needed to check their bits out. I laughed out loud, for what seemed like the first time in ages. It felt like an omen. I would pass these exams, and be a gynaecologist myself, one day. As a specialist, I would reach the third level of the hierarchy of hospital medicine - I had decided at Med School that student doctors kiss arse, junior doctors cover arse, and consultants kick arse. It would be a change to spend time at the top. Meanwhile I studied hard to put my arse-kicking feet firmly on the ladder to the top.

The day before the exam I took the tube to Baker Street station and walked to the Royal College of Obstetrics & Gynaecology where the exam was being held. It felt important to do a dummy run so I'd know how long to set aside the next day for travel. I revised my notes on the tube to the college. A man sitting opposite asked what I was up to. I said I had an exam the next day, and he said

"How lovely, to meet an Australian nurse. I've never been to Australia, you know."

He was so friendly that I didn't have the heart to correct him. Australian indeed!

The exam consisted of two two-hour multiple-choice papers, taken on the same day. The Royal College of Obstetrics & Gynaecology was situated on Regent's Park. The place was packed with candidates, most of them looking even more nervous than I felt. We were a multicultural group. As far as I could ascertain, I was the only Kiwi, but there were Africans and Asians, and many women in traditional Islamic dress.

We sat the papers in a large hall with individual tables set out in rows, like high-school exams. The chairs we sat on had the names of fellows of the Royal College carved into them. I recognised none of the names.

Before we started, I spoke to a young British doctor who said he'd done a couple of weeks' swot, and felt quite relaxed about the exam. I caught up with him again in the break after the first paper. He looked sick, and said he didn't think he'd bother sticking around for the next paper; he hadn't even understood some of the questions, and would work far harder before attempting it again.

He wasn't the only person to feel sick. The queue for the toilet reached out the door, and the smell of nervous diarrhoea was nauseating.

During the break between papers I strolled through Regent's Park, and considered asking another of the candidates if they'd go for a row on the lake with me. My courage failed, no one seemed friendly or approachable, so I wandered down the paths alone, listening to a 'Muttonbirds' tape on my Walkman.

The second paper was more difficult than the first, which I'd found easy. Perhaps I hadn't passed, but this wouldn't be shameful - fewer than ten percent of candidates pass their Part One examinations at the first attempt.

When I got back to the flat, a bunch of flowers from Bernard awaited me. John and Nicola had also brought flowers, which Bernard's Mum arranged in a crystal vase for me. We all had dinner together that night. It was a farewell meal, as John and Nicola were working the next day, and my flight was a day later. I was now completely relaxed with Bernard's parents and brother. They were welcoming and loving, and I felt like a part of their family already.

Lizzie, a medical student and friend of Bernard's family showed me around London the following day. I took photos of Buckingham Palace, and all the other touristy things through the windscreen of her car. A can of soft drink, sitting on the dashboard, obscures the detail in most shots.

Six weeks after the exam, the results were posted. I'd arranged to have my results sent to Bernard's family in Surrey, as then I'd hear the result a few days earlier than if I had to wait for them to reach New Zealand. By the time results came around, I was sure I'd failed the exam. I got home from work at ten-thirty one night, to a message on the answer phone. It was Bernard's Dad.

"Lauren, I'm sorry." There was a big pause. "I'm sorry

you're not there, as I'd like to tell you in person that you passed your exam. Congratulations, my dear."

I'd passed. I shrieked with joy.

Bernard was away on a rugby trip so I was home alone. I rang the hospital, and asked to speak to one of my friends who was working late. Kathy squealed her congratulations. She would sit her Part Ones in another six months. It was too late to ring anyone else. I barely slept that night.

I was working on a surgical run, and felt as though the floor was at least a metre below my feet as I floated through the next day. Congratulations abounded as the word spread. I now realised what a great achievement it had been. Everyone was proud of me for realising my goal. I was assured of a place on the Obstetrics and Gynaecology training scheme at Wellington Women's Hospital, my dream for the past two years. Despite the shambles of my son's life, and the recurring problem of my depression, it seemed that things were finally getting better.

12

C hris was now in Social Welfare care in Featherston, and a Family Group Conference was set down to discuss his future. His guardianship rested with the state, something I was pleased about. They could care for him, keep the community safe from him, and provide the counselling he so obviously needed.

The Family Group Conference took place in Featherston. Grandma, Bernard, my dad, police, social workers, Chris and I all sat in a small room like a classroom. An urn of tea and plate of sandwiches were produced, and the aims of the Family Group Conference written up on a whiteboard.

Chris looked sullen and small at the front of the room. He was excused after a while to wander off and let the adults decide his fate. He seemed pleased to leave. It didn't seem real that the young man at the centre of our discussion, the boy I'd given birth to only thirteen years earlier was the perpetrator of the crimes that were listed at the meeting. The social workers talked of theft, truancy, and sexually inappropriate behaviour. Chris had absconded from welfare care and spent a night in the cells after being found by police tracker dogs. He was not a happy boy, and needed a loving family environment. Bernard and I were a family. We could care for him.

I produced a letter from my psychiatrist to say I was unwell myself, and couldn't deal with the stress of caring for Chris in the immediate future. This was disregarded. Bernard and I knew, the moment the Family Group Conference began, that it had been decided that the appropriate placement for Chris was with us. We had a week to get things ready for him.

There was no choice. My health was not the concern of the authorities. They cared only that Chris was returned to his family, no matter how inappropriate that placement was. It wasn't the last bad decision they would make about his care.

We didn't want Chris living with us until he'd had some help. He didn't want to live with us either, but that was the decision of the Family Group Conference, and we abided by it. Not to do so would have made people believe we didn't care about Chris, and we did care what happened to him - we particularly wanted to be sure he received specialised help, and thought that being in the care of the state might hurry this along.

Shortly after the Family Group Conference, Chris made a statement to the Department of Social Welfare, and the Featherston police, to the effect that Terry, the kindly Christian camp leader, had sexually violated him. He withdrew this statement a few days later, saying he'd made it up.

Was his accusation a way of taking heat off himself for what he'd done to Melissa? I didn't think so. I believe Terry did abuse Chris, so I wanted to make sure that he was kept away from other young kids. I rang both St John's Ambulance and the Scout Association about Terry. Neither organisation seemed interested in the information I gave them. The Scouts said they could do nothing as Terry wasn't a 'real' Scout leader - he just helped them out from time to time. I was left with the impression that no one seemed to care about the kids who came into contact with this predator. No one would accept responsibility to take any action that would curtail Terry's actions in future.

The prodigal returned from Featherston, along with his unacceptable behaviour. I enrolled him at Wellington High School, after alerting the principal to his offending.

Although he started well there, within a week his behaviour became intolerable. He swore at and stole from teachers, walked out of classes, and had alarmed the principal by standing on a bank outside her office, and motioning as though he was going to throw himself off it. I'd certainly played up at school when I was his age, and knew that some of his behaviour was a reflection of his own inner sadness and anger. I tried to get to the core of what was bothering Chris, but he wouldn't open up to me. I felt helpless in the face of his turmoil. The level of his antics was of a far higher degree than mine had ever been, and I was extremely worried about him.

His nocturnal wandering to Grandma's resumed too. She continued her policy of neither confirming nor denying his arrival at her house, and of refusing to send him home. He was smoking heavily, and got the money to support this habit from Grandma. As he was too young to buy cigarettes himself, she'd trudge down to the dairy for him, spending her pension on his smokes. If she refused, he used standover tactics to get the cash he wanted. She still loved him unconditionally, the kind of love all kids need, but which I couldn't give him. To me, a young man who threatens an old woman and sexually abuses children is a hard person to love unconditionally.

13

I was now working at Wellington Women's Hospital as a Senior House Officer. I was doing the work I hoped to specialise in, working with women, their pregnancies and infants. It should have been a time of contentment, and fulfilment. It wasn't.

Chris was causing ongoing trouble. He was refusing to attend classes, was constantly rude to teachers, and would not follow the direction of the headmistress. He would make flamboyant gestures, hinting he was about to commit suicide, before storming out of the school grounds. The school would page me at the hospital to tell me what had happened. There seemed little the school or I could do. I left work early a few times to try to find him. I knew depression well, and wanted to be available to Chris if he was depressed or suicidal. It seemed he wasn't - he was just punishing everyone else for the pain and confusion he was feeling.

My early departures from work created big problems for the other junior medical staff. The women's health service was under-funded and under-staffed. Any absence, for whatever reason, caused added stress to the already overworked junior doctors. Our rostered hours were excessive even when we had a full complement of staff. A weekend duty for a registrar, coming once in every four or five weekends, began on a Friday evening and finished Monday after ward rounds, which could last until midday.

Complaints to our union were fruitless. We were in a difficult situation. If we wanted the training, we accepted the conditions. I wanted to specialise in obstetrics and gynaecology so I kept my head down as much as possible and did the work. My standards had slipped though. I was no longer willing to put in extra hours for the sake of my education. I literally had no extra hours in the day. Chris was at home - doing God knows what - for long periods when I was at work. Bernard couldn't cope with him, and I felt that Grandma shouldn't have to. I feared for the community with him on the loose. What more could I do to help him?

Working in the Delivery Suite brought me into contact with a number of frighteningly young women and their families. It was heartening to be able to reassure these people, based on my own experience, that teen pregnancy didn't have to mean an end to ambition or achievement. I told many that I'd had my first baby at seventeen. I didn't tell them about Chris's problems. Not only was it inappropriate, I knew that his problems were not due to my youth at the time of his birth.

Working so much with women and their babies made me think about my own mother, and the way I'd shut her out of my mind. My relationship with my Mum had been almost as full of turmoil as the one between Chris and me. I'd largely cut her out of my memory, having too much in my life now to deal with my feelings for someone who'd been dead for seventeen years. One night, exhausted after a sixty-hour shift, I had an amazing and cathartic dream that allowed me to reassess my relationship with my Mum, and make my peace with her. It also made me re-evaluate some of my judgement of Chris.

In the dream I was wearing a white doctor's coat and walking down a series of long white corridors in what was obviously a hospital. There were many doors - all closed, all unmarked - leading off the corridors, which turned in all directions. I could hear my rubber-soled shoes squeak on the grey linoleum of the passage I was on, and feel the blue linen skirt I was wearing touching the back of my calves.

I stopped at a door, indistinguishable from all the others, and entered without knocking.

Lying on the bed blindfolded and restrained at all limbs, was my mother. Her hair was copper, and the length it was when I last saw her, lying in her coffin. She was my patient. She turned her head towards me, knowing it was me at her side.

"Please let me go, Laurie. Please. I want to be free again, to go to the beach, to play like I used to. Remember the fun we had together, at the beach, Laurie? Remember the day I buried my money in the sand? What a good mother I was to you? Please untie me."

Mum begged me, weeping, and I started to cry with her. We both knew I possessed the authority to remove her bonds, but I wouldn't. I touched her arm. It was warm and alive.

"No Mum; you're sick. I can't let you go." Tears coursed down both our faces. She began to sob. I tried to be reasonable, professional.

"Mum, I can't do this for you. I'm sorry I wasn't a better daughter. I hated your friends, and the things they did to you, to us. I had to choose Grandma over you. I remember the day at the beach, when the waves came in and washed all the grocery money away, and you were mad because you wouldn't be able to buy smokes. We went without food that day, and you were upset about your cigarettes. Yes, I remember, Mum. If I could let you go now, to lie on the beach, to smell the grass, and know you would get better, I would. I can't, though. You have to stay here like this to get well. I'm sorry Mum."

It's true - I ached for her, and wanted to do whatever I could to help her, but the hard way seemed to be the best one.

I left the room, still crying. She had turned her back to me.

It was a hard thing to do, but I faced my Mum, and sorted some things out with her. I could now move on.

When I woke, it was with a feeling of utter peace, as though I had been relieved of a great burden while I slept.

The dream was as much about Chris and me as it was about my relationship with my Mum. It reminded me that I'd once preferred Grandma to my parents - so Chris's desire to be with her wasn't perhaps as disloyal as I'd been thinking.

14

I loved Bernard; on reflection I loved him almost as much as the idea of marrying him. My first marriage took place when I was eighteen, and was to a man I'd known for less than fifteen hours. I wore a pair of jeans and white singlet-top then. I wanted a real wedding: a dress-up one with presents, and guests, and photographs, and a groom that I loved, and knew well. Planning for a wedding would be fun, and might take my mind off all the stressful things that were going on in the rest of my life.

The planning was hugely entertaining, as was the anticipation of a whole day where Bernard and I would take centre stage. Gone was my fear that a traditional wedding would be an embarrassment or a cringe.

We bought clothes for my boys at Leod Hais, a trendy clothing store in Wellington. Paulie touched the female shop assistant on the breast as she was measuring him up for a waistcoat. She was upset, and told him that she didn't like boys touching her there. He smiled, and gave her an innocent look before asking her "Do you only like it when girls touch your breasts?"

Although we shouldn't have, Bernard and I began to laugh. Even the shop assistant seemed to think it was funny. Paulie giggled too, but I'm not sure he really understood what he'd said.

Bernard and I were married on 5 February 1994, in an

outdoor ceremony on a perfect day. Christopher gave me away, and read 'The Owl and the Pussycat'; I hoped his role in the ceremony would give him a sense of belonging in this new family. I wore a traditional wedding dress of champagne Dupion silk, and a veil, which I mostly kept off my face; I couldn't resist the odd virgin bride pose! My wedding dress, like the one I wore on my last day at Medical School, showed 'Roger', my dragon tattoo, perfectly.

Paulie was an attendant. Dressed identically to Chris, he picked his nose and rubbed at his crotch almost constantly, and always found the video or stills camera, so he could offer his grubbiest side to it. When Bernard and I kissed after exchanging vows, Paulie jumped between us, smooching my cheek. Everyone could hear his delighted cry "I married my Mum!"

'Temperature's Rising', an *a cappella* group, sang during the ceremony, and for the whole evening afterwards. Paul and my half-brother Tim joined the band members to sing along to 'My Girl'.

Chris was charm personified. Everyone commented on his good looks and impeccable manners. He assisted the older guests to their chairs, poured wine and distributed flowers to family members at the end of the evening. I was so proud of him. It seemed impossible that I could feel such pride and anger towards the same person.

Having ambivalent feelings for my son - the child I'd adored, and had promised the world to - saddened me. I wanted to be a good mother, but had failed. I thought at length about the modelling for parenthood I'd received from my own Mum and Dad, and began to understand why I mightn't fulfil the role well myself.

Bernard and I honeymooned in Dunedin with his parents, who had come over from England for the wedding. We travelled there by car, staying in Nelson and Akaroa on the way down. It was a wonderful trip, in no way less enjoyable because it was spent with the in-laws.

One of the nights in Akaroa we slept in a backpacker cabin. It was open plan, with a large living room downstairs and a mezzanine floor on which Bernard and I slept. His parents had the foldout couch downstairs for the night. It seemed a little awkward having sex in essentially the same room as his parents, but we thought we'd manage after they nodded off. After all, wasn't that the point of a honeymoon?

Our bed took up all the room on the tiny mezzanine. There was one light source, a lamp positioned just behind the headboard. The downstairs area was in darkness, and the in-laws asleep when we put our books down and started to make love. It was a hot evening, so we were on top of the blankets, knowing that due to the orientation of the floor we were on, we were invisible to Bernard's parents. Cautiously, we started, desperate to be quiet, but needing each other's touch. Bernard lay on his back, a superb erection between his thumb and forefinger, holding his wedding tackle perpendicular to his body so I could admire it. I lifted my head; sure I could hear a muffled giggle from downstairs. I listened carefully - there it was again - a distinctly feminine noise. I looked over the foot of the bed. Bernard's penis, splendidly backlit by the lamp at the bed head, had been projected, many times its normal size, onto the blank wall facing us, forming a giant shadow play for his Mum and Dad. His cock was so highly magnified it looked like a mushroom cloud. We turned the light off and giggled ourselves to sleep. I'm still not sure if his Mum did see the sights, or if the giggle I thought I'd heard was imagined.

15

Chris joined us a couple of days later, when we arrived in Dunedin. I wanted to show him the city he'd felt excluded from when I was doing my medical training, to try to ease some of the memories he had of our separation then. When I'd moved to Dunedin for the two years medical training there, Chris had elected to stay in Wellington with my Grandma. I'd only taken Paulie, then a baby, with me. Chris had always resented my leaving him in Wellington, even though he'd made the decision to stay, largely on the basis that life was sweet for him there.

This holiday didn't make things better between us, but at least it showed I was trying. It was also a chance for Chris to display his talent for deception. We hadn't booked rooms in Dunedin, believing there would be no difficulty finding a place to stay. A Masters Games event in the city had booked out almost all accommodation. We got a couple of rooms in the stable block at Larnach castle. When we went into the castle proper for breakfast the next morning, Chris introduced himself to the staff there. Later that day he went for a walk while we wandered in the gardens. The next morning when we went to breakfast, Chris was already in the dining room, operating the cash register. My little entrepreneur had got himself a job: fourteen years old, and already so skilful at charming people. He resigned his new position when he saw the look on my face. We left later that day, without finding out whether or not the money in the till balanced.

We returned to Wellington, Chris to high school and Bernard to varsity. My new husband was trying all the subjects he was remotely interested in, to decide what to major in. I returned to the hospital I was growing to hate. The magic of delivering babies was still there. Every time I assisted in the delivery of a new life my eyes would fill with tears at the promise each birth brought, and the joy and relief of the occasion. I loved that job; however the long hours of work and lack of support were wearing me down. There is an institutionalised cruelty in hospital medicine, with the junior doctors pushed as hard as they can be by consultants and management who seem to care little for their safety. The consultants had once worked hundred-hour-weeks, so they expected their registrars and house surgeons to show similar heroism.

My feelings for Chris were as confused as ever, as were his emotions towards me. It seemed wrong to feel such conflict towards someone you should be programmed to love - Chris and I both battled this ambivalence in our attitudes to one another.

The blues dragged me down again about a month after the wedding. Chris had been suspended from school, and was staying at home while I worked. He got himself invited into people's homes, and twice I was phoned by neighbouring women who wanted to adopt him into their families - containing small children - as they'd heard from him about our unhappy home life, and how I was too wrapped up in my work to care for him. He also told them I was a liar, and not to believe anything they heard from me about him. He was so convincingly 'nice', and I was so obviously a scheming, nasty bitch who hated her son. They fell for it.

Chris was quickly dropped from these 'new families' when I informed the women of his sexual offending, and told them that the police would confirm what I was saying.

I had to tell them they were about to admit a self-acknowledgedged paedophile into their homes, and that their children - however young, of whichever gender - would be unsafe with him there.

Chris was furious with me. This confirmed to him that I had it in for him, that I hated him, and that he would be better off living elsewhere. I didn't want him living with Grandma. Apart from his violence towards her, and the stealing, she refused to believe he had ever abused a child, so was unlikely to supervise his access to children. As I have multitudes of cousins with young kids, all of whom visited Grandma at times, it was not safe for him to live there.

I applied for, and was granted, stress leave, after explaining the problems I was having with Chris to one of the administrators. She was horrified and sympathetic about the situation I was in. My co-workers were dismayed at my cheek asking for time off. We were all so overworked that the illness or absence of another was only seen in the light of the extra duties it meant for those who were left on the roster. It was an impossible situation for all of us.

My wedding had made me a special friend. Cathy Dee was our photographer. She had a wicked sense of humour, and was just the antidote I needed to my flourishing depression. Cathy called a spade just that, and had a refreshing view of life. Added to that, she enjoyed my passion for lollies and champagne, and made me look really good on film. She was, truly, a girl's best friend. I loved her.

Most of the three weeks stress leave were spent with Cathy. We were both depressed and taking Prozac, and took to walking through the country village of Makara where she lived, making up stories and telling silly jokes. Laughing constantly, we found each other's company healing. We also spent stacks of money on sweets and alcohol, and probably ruined our teeth and frightened our livers forever. Cathy helped me remain sane in that difficult time. She also captured the wedding so beautifully that I relive it when looking at the photos. It was one of those rare days when everything felt perfect.

One night of my stress leave, Bernard and I went out to a dance recital, and were spotted by one of the other Senior House Officers from Wellington Women's. She glared at me. Her look seemed to say the least I could do, if I must avoid work, was stay at home and mope.

It seemed I could do nothing right. Perhaps obstetrics and gynaecology was not the best career choice for me. To do well at my job, I needed the support of my peers. I seemed unlikely to regain that now. The patients seemed to love me, but as often happens in hospital medicine, what they thought counted for little. I held on. I had too much invested to leave my job without another attempt at working it out. When my leave ended, I tried my hardest to keep everyone happy, but it was too late for that. My collegial support was evaporating. As hurtful as this was, I could understand it.

16

I t wasn't long before Chris was suspended again from
school for repeat truancy, theft and failing to follow
the teachers' instruction. Bernard and I tried to find an
alternative for him. At fourteen he was below the legal school-
leaving age, and was unsafe to be left without supervision. We
found him a place at the Activity Centre, a school for teens
who didn't fit anywhere else. He promised to attend there
every day, aware that this was his last chance of getting a high
school education without taking correspondence lessons -
something we all believed he wouldn't manage.

He was soon missing classes again, and threatened with
expulsion. At the end of our tolerance, Bernard and I sought
another Social Welfare placement for Chris, in an attempt
to keep him contained and the community safe from him,
while he received some help for his behaviour. He had been
having counselling at the Wellington Child and Family Clinic
for over a year, and his caseworker there had just twigged
that Chris was deceiving him. Although Chris projected an
air of regret for his actions, he did in fact, feel no remorse.
This became more apparent as his counselling progressed.
He had at last disclosed that the extent of his offending was
greater than he had first admitted, and that his victims had
included Jacquie's six-year-old son. This offending first came
to notice when the boy, Jamie, saw an advertisement for socks
in a local newspaper. The advert showed the rear view of a
man - naked except for a pair of socks - walking down a city

street. "Mum," asked Jamie, "does daddy make you suck on his dick? Chris makes me do it to him, and he does wees in my mouth. It tastes yucky." Jacquie was aghast, and initially disbelieved her son. For months Chris denied he'd touched the boy, only to reveal it when his case worker realised he'd been lying about other things.

He conceded that the children he abused were under the legal age for consent, but also said he only did things the children liked, and stopped when they asked him to. He did not admit to the threats he'd made to the kids to shut them up, nor to the gifts he gave them to ensure compliance. For such a young offender, Chris was experienced in the mechanics of abuse. He was frighteningly unaware of any moral wrongdoing, and seemed to feel the law was both unfair to those with his sexual predilections, and ill informed. He was, in the words of a senior policeman who spoke to me, a dangerous criminal. Apart from his attitude towards his offending, Chris was dangerous in that he seemed to be such a likeable young man. He was good-looking, articulate and seemed caring. He was the kind of boy some people would happily send their children off with, even after only one meeting with him.

17

While all this was happening, I was again distracted from my work. I was slow to learn new skills, especially the practical ones. In a surgical speciality such as obstetrics and gynaecology, quick learning of skills was essential. My colleagues were beginning to perform surgical procedures like Caesarian sections and sterilisations solo, where I still assisted a more senior doctor. I don't learn practical tasks instantaneously, as the others seemed to do, but by continued, supervised practice. This became a source of frustration to the senior staff, who had better things to do than baby-sit a doctor whose mind was elsewhere.

In other skills, such as communication, and empathy, I could hold my own with all of the others. These are skills that are difficult to quantify, though, and mattered most to the patient who was the recipient of them. No one else seemed to notice that I was the only junior member of staff on some shifts to assist women undergoing the termination of grossly abnormal pregnancies; for instance when severe birth defects were present. This meant I was called back to the hospital on my evenings off, to explain procedures and events to families who were intensely shocked and grieving at the lost of a much longed-for and loved baby. Many of the other junior staff were opposed to abortion, and wouldn't differentiate between ones performed solely for maternal reasons, and those for fetal abnormality - sometimes so gross the infant would never be capable of a life outside the womb. I despaired of the attitudes of some of them. Couldn't they see the anguish that the decision to terminate caused these women and their families?

I hugged a lot of women and their partners, dried copious tears, and delivered all too many dead fetuses that year. It was worthwhile, although painful work. The midwives appreciated my empathy with the women, and I was soon the junior doctor of choice for working with women who were delivering a baby who'd died unexpectedly before birth.

Although I'd never had a stillbirth or abortion myself, I seemed to have a natural empathy for women facing these experiences, and the women themselves greatly appreciated it. I think having a disabled child helped - knowing the difficulty of caring for an offspring with even mild to moderate disability helped me to understand the decisions these families had come to. Not one patient that I met in the Women's Hospital had reached their decision to terminate lightly, and all of the parents I saw and assisted were certain they were making the best choice from two unhappy options. It was not my role, nor that of the other staff, to stand in the way of these parents' legal right to opt for abortion. I'm sad that some of my colleagues saw fit to abandon the care of these extremely needy families.

After one of these abortions the midwives on the ward would ink the fetus's hands and feet, and make a card with tiny hand and foot-prints for the grieving parents. They would also take a Polaroid photo of the fetus wearing a little nightie or wrapped in a blanket, a fresh flower lying alongside it. A physical record of the event might help the parents with their grieving. If they didn't want these mementoes they were kept in the mother's medical notes so she could see them if she ever changed her mind.

One woman and I shared hugs, tears and the odd rude joke while she was delivering a severely deformed fetus with no hope of life beyond the womb. The next day she brought me a couple of cakes shaped like breasts, as she'd noticed my surgical scrub top was more than amply filled. I was amazed that even in the midst of her own pain she could still find a sense of humour.

18

The most challenging aspect of the obstetrics and gynaecology work was the surgery. My commitment to my patients wouldn't allow me to attempt a task by myself unless I knew I was up to coping with any adverse consequences that might occur. It can take only a short time to learn how to perform a minor operation, but many years to learn all the skills to cope with the consequences if something goes wrong. I knew gynaecological anatomy well, having learned it for the Part Ones - my theoretical knowledge wasn't the problem. My distractedness and slowness to pick up some of the skills let me down, and my growing anxiety about my deficiencies only made things worse. Stress and depression were eroding my self-confidence.

The operating theatre I loved. The performance of skilled work, the dressing up, the atmosphere, and the sense of privilege that I'd been entrusted with the task of performing an operation on someone, were exhilarating. As I acquired more skills, my confidence grew and I enjoyed it more. But the spectre of Christopher followed me wherever I went, even into the rarefied atmosphere of the operating theatre. Where was he? What was he doing? Who was he hurting this time?

There was also the constant reminder that others on the training scheme were far ahead of me in 'operation counts', and the feeling that I was disliked by a few of them, for not pulling my weight. I tried, I tried so hard - there was just too much happening in my life. At a time in my training where I needed utter dedication and commitment to my work, I was unable to give this. It wasn't the way I wanted to do things; it was simply the way things were.

The Social Welfare Department finally found a placement for Chris. He was to live with a family who had cared for other troubled kids, to see if they could normalise his behaviour in a more controlled environment. Their home was in Island Bay, only a couple of kilometres from our flat. Chris had to pass our place to get to school or town. I still felt extremely vulnerable to attack by him, even though he was no longer living in our house. His anger at me showed no sign of abating and I had become so frightened of him I'd had a lock placed on the inside of my bedroom door - I wanted to avoid nasty surprises in the middle of the night. Constant fear made me exhausted.

When rostered on overnight (10pm to about 9am), Senior House Officers were required to be awake for the whole shift, whether we were busy or not. There was a sleeping room, just off the delivery suite, but this was declared out of bounds during the night shift. If we disobeyed this directive we were reprimanded in front of the others the following day. I was exhausted; more from constant fear than overwork, and did sleep, if not in the Senior House Officers' room then on the floor in one of the common rooms. I had my pager, and was less than a minute away from Delivery Suite, so felt this was a safe compromise: safer than staying awake when my nerves were so jangled. I wasn't sleeping during the day, because of the combination of exhaustion and worry. I felt so vulnerable in the house by myself. My body was constantly on alert. The slightest noise sent my heart racing and filled my mouth with the taste of fear. I was tired and wired, scarcely a winning combination.

My next run was to be a three-month attachment to the

Neonatal Unit, a prospect that daunted me. I was the last obstetrics and gynae Senior House Officer to be obliged to spend three months in the unit - the neonatologists and paediatricians had become aware of the amount of stress this attachment caused - both to the SHO, and to the neonatal department itself. Three months in a specialised unit is not long enough to learn the requisite skills, and since most SHOs didn't want to continue with a career in hospital medicine, the run was unnecessary and resented by some of them. I was utterly miserable. My life was a mess, my chosen career wasn't looking as promising as it once had, and I was expected to care for minuscule scraps of life; using machines and tiny devices I couldn't name, let alone operate. The nurses were wonderful, but it was soon apparent to the staff of the unit that they had a klutz in their midst. I spent hours crying in a cupboard, hoping and praying that someone would rescue me. I was having a terrible crisis of confidence, and pleaded with the paediatricians and the obstetricians to let me return to delivery suite, to work that I understood, and still loved, but they refused. In my last month of neonates I was assigned a more senior doctor to baby-sit me during night shifts. Although reassuring, this was extremely humiliating. What was I doing here?

I now had a better idea of how to resuscitate a sick or tiny infant, an essential skill for an obstetrician. I was still so unconfident though that if a baby born by Caesarean section needed an airway tube inserted, I would ask the anaesthetist for help. God, I felt inadequate. I wish this training had come at a better time for me. Perhaps then I could have avoided the problems that followed.

19

Bernard and I celebrated our first wedding anniversary with a night at the Parkroyal Hotel in Wellington. One of my Med School classmates had given us a night in the hotel as a wedding present, so our first night as an official couple had been spent there. Bernard was in his second year at Victoria University, where he was studying Maori, history and maths. I was learning te reo Maori too, as an extramural student at Massey University. My Maori studies were going really well; I consistently got A's. It was important to my self-esteem to be performing well in one area of my life. And it felt right to be able to greet my Maori patients in their own tongue.

Bernard gave me a tiki carved from whalebone as my anniversary gift. I hadn't bought him anything. I wore the tiki - a fertility symbol - to my work at Wellington Women's. It had another symbolism for us: I'd had a sterilisation operation during Med School and we planned for me to have the tubal ligation reversed. Perhaps a baby of our own would be something to strive for. I didn't stop to think that I had quite enough stress in my life without adding to it. I had also not yet proven that I could be a good mother; a baby then could have been another disaster. Fortunately we never did get around to conceiving, despite practising hard.

For the first time in my life, I was enjoying the winter. It was usually the time of year when my depression overwhelmed me. On Saturdays my rugby doctoring gave me something stimulating to do, even though it sometimes meant shivering on the sidelines in the sleet. Our team had amalgamated with the Victoria University side, and was now called Harlequins. I attended every match, but was excused practice evenings. Part way through the season I started bringing my own drink bottle to the games. The boys had their water bottles by the field - now I had one too, a pink one. Mine didn't have water in it - the team knew that they would get a mouthful of gin and tonic if they drank from the pink bottle, so they never did. The gin in the pink bottle was an allusion to the team's nickname. For many years the Wellington College Old Boys side had been known as 'the pink ginners'. I drank little, as I needed to be able to deal with any emergency that happened, and there were a few. One of the Harlequins' players was eye gouged quite severely; another had a heart attack on the field. There were numerous lacerations, a few dislocated shoulders and knees, and some nasty concussions. Sometimes even spectators became patients. One elderly man collapsed while watching a game, and I sent him off in an ambulance with a suspected stroke. No, the gin and tonic on the sideline was there for fun rather than need.

The saddest time I had caring for the team came when one talented young player committed suicide. Cookie hanged himself one night after a party at our flat. He'd seemed elated - the happiest we'd seen him in ages. None of us stopped to think that perhaps his happiness came from the decision he'd made to end his earlier sadness by taking his own life. None of us realised he was still depressed, and the team and supporters found his death incomprehensible. His funeral, at St Paul's, was the biggest I've ever attended.

Paulie came to some rugby games with us, if he was staying those weekends. At a game at the Basin Reserve, the Harlequins' home ground, he ran eight laps before stopping. His energy was admirable. At another ground he entered the sawdust gym and turned on a fire hose, flooding it. Punishment didn't work with Paulie - he seemed to forget it before the next opportunity to wreak havoc. Added to his obsession with water was one with electrical sockets. Bernard and I took him to Wellington Zoo one Sunday, and Paulie noticed all of the taps and power points in the cages. It was as though the animals didn't exist. Paulie couldn't tell if something was alive or battery-operated. On seeing a dead cat in the gutter near our home, he urged me to buy some batteries for it to make it go again. He was nine.

20

Despite my less-than-sterling performance as a Senior House Officer, I received an appointment the following year as a registrar at Wellington Women's Hospital. This was a more senior position, and involved longer hours of work and greater responsibility. I felt at once excited and fearful about my new role. Excited because it meant that the senior doctors thought I was coping okay with the job even though I lagged behind others on the training scheme; fearful because I was all too aware of my inadequacies.

Things were no better at home. I was exhausted, but having trouble sleeping. Chris had threatened to kill the people he was staying with in Island Bay, and his position there was unlikely to continue. He was on the brink of expulsion from the activity centre, and had threatened to trash my house. I was fearful that he would burn it down one day. Bernard and I changed the locks. Still, at the end of every shift I worried about what kind of mess I would return home to. Walking home, I imagined that any police car or fire engine in the street was going to a disaster at my place.

One day I had the idea to help myself to a sleeping tablet from work. Temazepam, a weaker relative of Diazepam (Valium), was the sleeping drug of choice for pregnant women and those who had just delivered. It is quick acting and not addictive if taken for short periods, on an as-required basis. There were bottles of it on each of the three wards of the Women's Hospital, and it was ridiculously easy to access. It worked wonderfully. As it works rapidly, I took it on my way home from work, and was ready to sleep when I got there. I woke at the end of a long sleep, with no residual drowsiness. This was amazing. I began to feel positive. My work felt as though it was improving, too, as my fear and tiredness were lessening.

After a week of taking one sleeping pill most days, I found I needed a bit more. The sleep was now not so deep, and it needed to be if I was to function well. In addition, Chris had been expelled both from the place he was living at and the Activity Centre. He was with Grandma again, as he refused to live with us. Grandma said that things were "fine," although I heard from a trusted cousin that she had relinquished her chequebook and auto-bank card to one of her daughters, as Chris was hassling her for money. She was looking frail and had severe angina. She was soon hospitalised, and had a cardiac pacemaker inserted. The period in hospital at least took her out of the environment in which Chris reigned over her.

These worries entitled me to more Temazepam, I felt, to help me sleep off the effects of the long hours of work and the worries in my personal life. I took two after the next night shift, and kept another two by my bed in case I woke during the day. The sleep was a godsend. All the pills were gone when I woke, although I couldn't remember taking the second lot.

I didn't approach my own doctor about my sleep problems and stress levels - this seemed like something I could handle on my own. Besides, I knew he wouldn't have approved of the way I was dealing with things. I was ashamed, too, of not coping. The other doctors on my ward coped.

Soon I was taking a handful of pills as I walked home from the night or weekend shift. I'd keep another handful or a full bottle of them by my bed. I slept well, yet managed to answer phone calls if required - the only problem was, I had no recollection of what the call was about, or even that it had occurred. My good friend Cathy Dee rang me one rare pill-free day and started telling me how the injuries from her motorbike crash were healing. What crash? We'd apparently spoken about it at length a couple of days earlier. I'd sounded tired on the phone, but otherwise okay to her. How many other calls had there been?

I was okay though. I only ever took the pills at home, never at work, or before work. I had it under control. I was not endangering anyone; or so I kept trying to convince myself.

One thing I was noticing at work was that I was really irritable by the end of a 60-hour weekend shift - edgy, bad-tempered, strung out. I didn't stop to consider these might be manifestations of withdrawal. Hell no. Anyone would be tired working the hours I was.

My distress was becoming apparent to people outside the women's health service. Those I worked with thought I was distracted, and not up to being a Registrar. They were too stressed and busy themselves to see that I was falling apart.

One morning I walked home through the Medical School and was stopped in the car park by Eru Pomare, the Professor of Medicine, a man for whom I had great regard.

He hugged me, then held me at arm's length and smiled.

"Don't give up, Lauren. This place needs more doctors like you. Never forget that."

Tears filled his eyes and mine.

"Thanks Prof, thank you so much."

I didn't see Prof Pomare again. Two weeks later he died suddenly while on a tramping expedition with his wife. His final words to me became a mantra that has helped me through all my days as a doctor since.

At his tangi and burial I was stunned, as were so many others, that this great man - so young, so fit looking - had died. He is buried above Hongoeka Bay; I still visit him when I need to make some sense of the world.

Despite Professor Pomare's words of encouragement, I still needed my pills. I wish I'd had the wisdom to talk to him about my problems, as I know he would have given me the advice and guidance I so badly needed.

21

Chris continued to cause disruption. A friend phoned me to say he had an eleven-year-old boy staying with him. Grandma refused to believe there was any harm in letting the child stay at her house. After all, she made sure they were sleeping in separate beds. The police questioned the boy's mother, who was happy for him to stay with Chris, even when told he was a paedophile. The cops removed the child back to his mother's house, and demanded that Chris keep away from him. I appealed to the Social Welfare Department for assistance. Chris was obviously abusing again. They continued to say there were no places available where he could be contained.

This time I got assistance from my cousin Jacquie's husband, who phoned his Member of Parliament saying he'd go to the newspapers about the Department's ineptitude unless something was done.

Within twenty-four hours, Chris was in Dunedin at a Social Welfare home, where he was promised counselling about his sexual offending, and the abuse that Terry had subjected him to.

With Chris away from Wellington I felt safer. I pushed myself harder at work, and was beginning to perform without distraction. I still needed my little helpers to sleep, though … dozens of them. I truly believed I had things under control, and that there was no problem, as my use of the pills was confined to home. Although Bernard was aware that I was sleeping a lot, he assumed it was because of the hours I was working.

We bought a house in Newtown. I was on a chunky salary, and had fallen in love with a little townhouse just across the road from the hospital. It was a convenient place to live while working such long hours. After taking my sleeping pills on the way out the Delivery Suite door, all I had to do was stumble a few hundred metres down and across the road, then straight into bed. In the new place Bernard and I had separate study areas, and there was room for Paulie to stay with us in the weekends, or Chris if the need arose.

Another of the registrars I was working with had become disenchanted with Wellington Women's Hospital, and relocated to National Women's in Auckland. He and I talked for hours about the stresses of the job, and he felt I, too, would be better off out of the hospital where I was working.

It was becoming clear that the rigours of the training scheme were too much. I was not the right person to become a specialist. This had been hammered home to me by one of my consultants who told me that doctors had no place hugging patients. I had "confused the doctor and nurse role," and would be the laughing stock of any overseas hospital with my attitude to patients. It was time for me to get real about my future.

One morning I decided that I needed to get out of the hospital system. Citing my mental health as the reason for my resignation, I walked away giving no notice. It was a pattern I had followed often in my life, to hang on until things were unbearable, then walk away when it was too late to work things out. Leaving others to pick up the pieces after me.

I was unemployed. More significantly, although I didn't click at the time, I had lost my supply of Temazepam. It was time to stop using it anyway - who needed a brain-full of drugs when they were no longer working in such a stressful environment?

That night I didn't sleep so well. There were only two capsules left, found after a frantic search through my bag after lying awake most of the night. They made no discernible difference. This wasn't surprising, as I'd been taking literally dozens of them every day for several weeks. Where did the pharmacist think they were going?

For 48 hours I didn't sleep at all. The third night my thoughts were racing. I felt I was going mad: I was twitchy, dizzy, and extremely frightened. If I held a full glass, the fluid trembled out of it. There was a sense of being hyper-alert. Every noise made me jump with fear, my mouth was dry and my heart fluttered in my chest. My speech raced almost as fast as my thoughts. I felt manic - perhaps I'd crossed the border between sad and mad. The fear of being really crazy fed my panic. I paced distractedly around the house, disturbing Bernard's sleep. The gulf between us was widening with the stress, drugs, and my concern about his long-term status as a hard-up student.

Next morning I made an urgent appointment to see my psychiatrist, who diagnosed benzodiazepine withdrawal. He wasn't sure what to do with me, as it was likely that I'd passed the worst of the withdrawal process. Complicating his decision was my inability to tell him how many drugs I'd been taking and how long I'd been abusing them. As I was so twitchy he decided to place me on a reducing dose of Valium to lessen the chances of my having epileptic fits related to the withdrawal. I was not allowed to work for a few weeks, and needed close observation for the next two to three days. Bernard stayed at home with me. He was supportive, yet stunned at the mess I had made of myself.

I had blood tests to check on my liver function, and was to see the psychiatrist again the following day.

I was relieved and ashamed. Although I was not going

mad as I'd feared, I was, truly, my mother's daughter … an addict. I should have known better. It was reassuring to know I wasn't crazy. This revelation was enough to slow my mind and speech a little.

22

The next few days I lay around at home, reading, resting, and thinking about the future. My stupidity in abusing and becoming addicted to self-prescribed medication was barely forgivable. How could I have been so thick? I wanted to be a doctor, but had behaved in a way that could lose me all rights to practise. I vowed to never again behave in such a brainless way. Meanwhile I needed to find more work.

The rugby doctoring was heaps of fun, but didn't bring in enough money to pay the bills. To continue it, I'd need to find work in another medical area to supplement the rugby income. Perhaps I could become a GP. I bought a textbook on general practice, and set about changing my goals. General practice frightened me - I'd have to know something about everything, but I had a few weeks to learn a bit more about the field. The textbook allayed most of my fears. I'd learned some of the skills I needed already, in the hospital and on rugby fields around New Zealand.

I spent the week after finishing the course of Valium applying for locum general practice work. My psychiatrist cleared me for work, and was satisfied that I'd learned my lesson. There was a lack of locums with spare time, so I soon found there was plenty of work available, even for an inexperienced GP. It was heartening that some of the doctors I thought were the best in Wellington wanted me to look after their patients. There was work available further afield too. I was asked to

Detail of the Celtic/Maori pattern on my arm, tattooed by Roger Ingerton

PHOTO BY GRAHAM

'Petal', 1982

A touch of Glamour

Christopher at age 11

CONTACT

JULY 8, 1999

Contact is Wellington's regional weekly and New Zealand's third-largest circulation newspaper. Read by 170,000. Delivered free.

Stripper, Prostitute, Doctor

By ROSS HENDERSON

THEY'RE not the sort of credentials likely to appear on most doctors' CVs: torn prostitute, fire-eating stripper, depressive, bankrupt.

But for Kapiti GP Lauren Roche, her experiences in the school of hard knocks were every bit as valuable as the skills learnt at medical school.

That background has given her more empathy with people and made her a better doctor, she says.

She has written about her past in an autobiography, tentatively titled Bent But Not Broken, set to be released later this year.

It begins with a childhood spent on the road with her two sisters, their mother, her boyfriend and his three children in Australia.

Most of the time was spent

But when Lauren was 14, her mother committed suicide — an experience she describes in the book.

"Mum died 22 years ago and I'm at last becoming aware of her as a person, she was flawed, sad, special and full of need."

When Lauren is sad or lonely, she still thinks of her.

"Although at times she was an appalling mother, she's the only one I had, and I know she loved me."

There were many sides to her mother. She was the woman who woke her to listen to thunder and who danced in the rain. She was the fearless climber of mountains and the mother who staggered drunkenly down the street to escape her children.

ing caught and sent home.

Then she threatened she was pregnant. Aged 17 with no prospects, she found work as a fire-eater in a strip club.

When her son Christopher was born, she went on the DPB and tried to straighten things out.

But it was a struggle.

She was soon back on the streets, this time working in a massage parlour.

Eight months later she became a prostitute. "One day I just thought 'Bah, there's all this money'. The secret to surviving was just to have your head on another level while you were doing it and think about the money."

Two years on Vivian Street took its toll.

Severe depression led to a

The 'Contact' article

With my Dad, Tracey and Shelley, February 1994. Having my Mum there would have made the day perfect.

Paulie 'marries' his Mum and Bernard.

With my two boys.

Larnach Castle
(we stayed in the stable block)

y house in Raumati looked out at Kapiti Island, a source of inspiration and strength for so
any people on the coast. It was devastating to lose it.

With Frank at my first
Devotion dance party

No parent would want their child to be in any way connected with such a headline.
REPRINTED COURTESY *Evening Post*

Make your first
appointment
after
Devotion '97

Dr Lauren Roche
M.B.Ch.B
DIP.OBS
Ph:

Cathy Dee photos at the time I w[as]
opening my new surgery. The one
used in the ad at left is actually
from a series about depression,
hence the black clothes and the
skull. This was the only one I was
smiling in. Cathy's black dog Sno[w]
was in all the photos.

The two Napoleons, Grant and Tony, at the GALA Ball, 1997.

The cast of Kapiti Players production of 'Out Of Order' - Bethany Adams, Michael O'Hagan, Murray Adams, Rhys Miller, Rob Heather, me, Colin Payne and Liz Kaye

JOHN BOCOCK

A publicity shot for Kapiti Playhouse Theatre's production of Out of Order in April 2000. I played Nurse Foster, who gives the 'kiss of life' to George Pigden (Murray Adams).

Replica guns will see someone shot – police

By NEIL REID
Crime reporter

PAINT WARS – Troy Taylor, at rear, and Chris Roche with the paint-guns which sparked an armed police alert at a public park in Petone. Picture: ROSS GIBLIN

Police see red over paint-gun fun

Two youths playing with paint guns sparked an armed police alert yesterday in Petone.

Armed police and a dog handler converged on to Hikoikoi Reserve, Marine Parade, after a person reported seeing two people running around with guns.

They found Chris Roche and Troy Taylor armed with paint guns purchased the previous week for $100 each. Mr Roche said he knew something was wrong when he saw a police officer trying to open the door to his car.

"They were calling the armed offenders squad out and they had to call them off," he said.

"We were just out there having the first proper play with them.

They like police were worried because the Mongrel Mob has a pad nearby.

"Nothing came of it. Bon them. I would definitely support that, it is going to save a life somewhere along the way."

Police National Headquarters operations head Superintendent Neville Matthews said police were considering whether imitation firearms and airguns should come under the same import controls as all other firearms.

This was still at an early stage and there would be consultation before any change. Registration of firearms was being considered by the Thorp review of firearms licensing and control, and it was not appropriate to comment on this until the review had been reported on in Parliament, he said.

Mr Matthews said concerns that presenting fake weapons could result in someone being shot were valid. But before police shot someone, they had to believe there was a real threat of death or grievous bodily harm and that the incident could not be resolved in a less violent manner.

Imitation guns now come under the same rules as airguns.

People aged 16-18 have to have a firearms licence if they are to use an imitation gun. Youths under 16 are allowed to have an imitation firearm only if they are supervised by someone permitted to own a real weapon.

Gun researcher Philip Alpers said police had investigated at least 240 incidents involving imitation firearms in the past two years. He had compiled the data from newspaper reports.

"Every single week there are one or two articles about local arms officers (and) arms sergeants holding two guns; one is the police issue Glock and (the other) an imitation gun," Mr Alpers said.

Last Wednesday a 12 year old boy used an imitation gun to challenge an Invercargill officer, sparking a toll-route armed offenders alert.

Auckland police last week called for the imitation guns to be banned after teenagers playing in a residential street sparked another armed offenders callout.

On Monday police took two youths from a car at gunpoint after an Eketahuna burglary. Police said the youths risked being shot, as they had a rifle and a replica of a Glock pistol.

July incidents in Wellington include three arrests at Wellington Railway Station, a Newtown youth arrested for allegedly pointing a firearm at passersby and four youths arrested in Porirua for playing with the guns in public.

Police Minister Jack Elder has met Police Headquarters staff to discuss the issue of fake guns.

Chris made the front page of the Evening Post
REPRINTED COURTESY *Evening Post*

Celebrating my birthday in the Coronary Care Unit a few days after the suicide attempt

SHARON ELLIOTT

My son Paulie's first day at high school

Paulie with Brewser.

KIRSTY SHIPP

With Wayne and Barnaby at the radio awards,
with Transgender Barbie and Lipstick Lesbian
Barbie.

Alan Duff at the Auckland Writers
Festival 2000 — he's a softie at heart

Helen Clark: I love the smile
— perhaps she should always
travel with a Barbie.

Brian Edwards put us both
at our ease and was great
for book sales.

Paul Holmes gave an
exclusive audience at his
1999 Christmas party

Nandor Tanczos high-fives
Dreadlock Barbie at the Auckland
Writers Festival 2000

Patriot Barbie at the Waiouru
Army Museum.

Steve, Tony, Wayne and Trevo with THAT book. The Dome, 5 November 1999

Alan Tristram at the Kapiti launch of Bent No Broken at Green House Books, 6 November 199!

above left: Speaking at the Auckland women's book weekend October 2000.
PHOTO COURTESY CAROLE BEU, WOMEN'S BOOKSHOP, PONSONBY.

above right: Outside Mt Crawford prison with Amanda Millar, who produced 'The Naked Doctor' —TV3's 20/20 programme on me and my son.
VIDEO STILL COURTESY TV3.

left: The Levin sexual health team: Gavin, Tracey, Lauren and Kate

work in three or four practices in Paraparaumu, both as a short-term locum and with the option of staying on as a partner if I fitted well into an existing practice.

I loved the Kapiti Coast. The weather was better, the beaches cleaner, and the people - with the exception of a couple of the doctors - friendlier than those in Wellington City. I wanted to relocate. Bernard wasn't keen. We had our townhouse in Newtown, and his parents were due to join us in a few months for our second anniversary. He enjoyed living in Wellington - it was closer to the university, where he was still a long way from completing his interminable degree. I once made a rude comment about the number of years he'd wasted mucking around at varsity (he'd already spent two years at Hull University in England). He countered that by saying at least unlike me, he hadn't spent years fucking strangers. A big bit of my love for him died then.

I spent five weeks in Paraparaumu over Christmas. Bernard stayed in Wellington. I relished the freedom and the isolation, while missing my little house. I read, lay in the sun, walked for hours, and practised medicine in a congenial and supportive atmosphere. I was in a three-doctor practice, filling in for someone who was on holiday. The second doctor also took a break of a few days, and during this time, the third partner became sick, leaving me in sole charge of the practice. I had to do call every night for four nights until one of the other local doctors stepped in to help. It was a tiring, though valuable experience. I coped, with no panic, no mistakes, and no recourse to drugs or alcohol. I was well again. Paulie spent some time with me, and welcomed the change of scenery too.

At the end of my time there, I returned to Wellington to consider a job offer on the Coast.

Christopher, described in a report as a "bright, charming

young man, with lots of potential," was released from the Social Welfare home in Dunedin after a few months. He returned to Grandma's to live. I saw him frequently. He'd had some counselling, and I felt it was time I tried to see his potential, and let go of the fears of the past. He assured me he would never again have sexual relations with anyone under the age of sixteen.

I bought a car - Priscilla - a black Nissan, and learned to drive. As a locum, I needed easy transport, as I was spending too much time on buses and trains.

Bernard and I separated, a week after our second anniversary, in a row in front of his parents, about how many more years he'd spend at university. In a flamboyant gesture, I swallowed my wedding ring - "My marriage has turned to shit, this might as well, too." It was eight days before I could retrieve it. After a thorough scrub, it looked shinier than ever, but the relationship had no such chance of redemption. I was sorry that I hadn't been able to make it work, even after five years of practice living together prior to our 2-year hitch. We sold our house, and I bought a new one in Raumati South. I had work available up there and an offer of an assistant-with-a-view job at the practice where I'd done the most locum work.

It was time for another new start.

23

My new house was a dream fulfilled. The mortgage on it was huge, but I was confident I could repay it. It had two storeys and four bedrooms, and perched on top of a ridge where it had vast views of the sea, and both Kapiti and Mana islands. Through the windows at the rear of the house, across the top of my garden, I could see the bare hills and paddocks to the east of Paraparaumu. My grounds were landscaped and planted with magnolias, camellias, rhododendrons, hibiscus, Mexican orange blossom and pohutukawa trees among others. There were shady patches filled with violets - pink, mauve and deep purple, all dripping with scent. I had two strawberry patches, a herb garden, a grape vine, fruit trees and a rockery planted with ferns which sheltered in the shade of the house. Although she'd never owned her own home, my Mum had created and tended gardens in some of the rentals we'd lived in. Both of my grandmothers were keen gardeners too. I relished the chance to tend my own patch of heaven on earth.

I couldn't believe my luck. Every morning, on waking, I'd open the curtains and see the outlook afresh, never quite believing that this spectacle was mine. I'd then walk barefoot into the garden, the grass wet with dew, a pair of scissors or secateurs with me to cut violets or daphne for a vase in the lounge. After putting the coffee on I'd walk down the steep drive to collect the morning paper. Then with coffee beside me I would finish the cryptic crossword in bed, looking out at

Kapiti Island solely to prove it was still there, that this wasn't just some delicious dream.

Having deferred paying tax in my first year as a self-employed locum, I had a huge tax bill. The Inland Revenue Department allows this practice in the first year of a new business. Along with some of the tax from my second locum year it was now all due. Never mind - it could wait till I'd bought new curtains for my house, and furniture for some of the rooms. I'd had a rough time, and needed to treat myself. Oh, the twisted thinking.

24

Chris stayed with me occasionally, along with a young man he introduced as his boyfriend. He seemed happy and more at ease than I'd seen him in a long time. Damon, the boyfriend, was a year older than Chris. He was tall and slim with sandy-blond hair, and was polite and good-looking. He and Chris made a handsome couple. They could have been mistaken for Mormon missionaries when together, until seen close-up, when their youth and the stink of tobacco dispelled those impressions. Damon and Chris stayed a few times at my house, in the queen-sized bed downstairs. I'd wake to the smell of cigarettes and socks and farts, hard to endure in my clean house.

The boys were always deferential, but rarely helpful - their promises to dig the vege garden were never kept. I still didn't trust Chris enough to leave him unsupervised in my house, but did allow him to be there if I was home. Things seemed fine. My medical work was fulfilling and enjoyable, my house and garden were beautiful, I was single and free, and it seemed my once-wayward teenage son was making an effort to be respectable. I had bought some exercise equipment, including a motorised treadmill, and had turned the third big bedroom into a gym. I would walk quickly on my treadmill for thirty minutes every day, while gazing out at Kapiti Island. Things were so rosy it was surreal. I would look out of my bedroom window at the sea, then closer, at my garden, my gleaming black car. It was hard to believe it all belonged to me.

Chris and Damon came to visit one Saturday with news. They'd found God, and were attending a church in Paraparaumu. I could feel the tilt of my eyebrow as they told me this. It couldn't be real. They had the earnest look of the newly converted though - perhaps it was true. With my own see-saw background, and coming from a Salvation Army family, I could hardly begrudge someone else his or her own transformation. I tried to bury my scepticism, and gave them the same message I'd given my sisters - be as religious as you like - just don't try to convert me. I'm not interested.

Chris and Damon attended church every week, travelling from Wellington to the coast, and visiting me after the service. I didn't ask whether they had disclosed their sexuality to the pastor or congregation, and they didn't offer this information. One day they brought three boys aged around 8 to 13 home with them. They were cousins whose families attended the same church; Chris and Damon had offered to take them out for a couple of hours to give their parents a break. I tried to ignore my disquiet about this development, and made sure the boys all stayed together, or were in my sight the whole time they were in the house. A gay friend of mine, Mark, was visiting too. I mentioned my misgivings to him; he understood my anxiety, but reminded me there had been no evidence that Chris was still sexually interested in children. Besides, he had a boyfriend now - a legitimate outlet for his hormones. It still didn't feel right, but I had to let go of the past and allow Chris the space he needed as a healthy young male. I went upstairs with Coke for the boys. Chris and Damon were playing on the treadmill with the younger kids - Damon had a video camera and was filming them as they ran, shirtless, on the machine. There was excitement in the air. I poured Cokes for the younger boys, and called Chris and Damon into the kitchen.

"I don't like the feeling of what's happening here, guys. Is anything going on with those kids?"

Chris looked at me as though he feared for my sanity. I

addressed Damon.

"Do you know Chris has had problems with kids before?"

He looked at the floor, running the toe of his shoe along a cut in the lino.

"Yeah, he told me. But that was a long time ago. He wouldn't do that any more. Anyway, he's got me now."

Chris glared at me. "Can we get back to our friends now? Don't worry, I won't be bringing them back here."

They left the room. Mark shrugged. "I know why you did that, but I don't think you need to worry."

The boys left. I knew their Christian names and recalled being doctor to one of them when I was a locum. It shouldn't be too hard to get the information I needed to warn their parents that my son and his 'boyfriend' might not be as benign as they seemed.

25

Grandma and I spoke regularly. She was pleased that I was spending more time with Chris. He was now living at Damon's parents' house in the Hutt. Grandma only saw him if he wanted money or some other favour.

Paulie stayed with me most weekends, and seemed to love his new 'second home'.

Aunty Trish (Mum's younger sister) and Grandma visited me occasionally. I was so proud of my house and garden, and loved to hear their praises about it, and to dig up or cut plants for them to take home. The house and gardens were my reward for the years of hundred-hour weeks, but I still worried that I didn't really deserve it all. My Mum had never owned a home, and Dad had bought his first place only a few years earlier.

My work was rewarding. I was seeing a large number of patients. People liked consulting a doctor who listened to them, and many of them transferred their files to me. This caused bitterness with another woman doctor in the area who saw it as a competition that she was losing. I saw it as patient choice in action.

The only part of my life that wasn't fulfilling at this time was the romantic one. My social contacts all revolved around work - the only people I was meeting these days were patients and colleagues, and I knew better than to dally with either of those sets. I was horny, too. The last time I'd had sex with someone else was several months earlier, and DIY sex was becoming predictable and boring. During this period of abstinence I realised my sexual fantasies had changed. I no longer wished for a man in bed with me - my feelings were, without exception, for women. I tried to analyse this. Perhaps I sympathised with Tallulah Bankhead who said "I don't know what I am, dahling. I've tried several varieties of sex. The conventional position makes me claustrophobic. And the others either give me a stiff neck or lockjaw." My sexual dealings with men were extremely complicated, starting with the rape at eight, and including the prostitution. Was this shift in my focus related to the traumas of the past? After all, the sex I'd had with women had always been consensual and enjoyable. I thought back over relationships I'd had, and attractions I'd felt as I was growing up. The boys I'd desired as a teenager had always been effeminate - slightly built, long-haired, sweet natured. My relationship with Paul had been intensely sexual, but it was complicated by the dual excitements of his being a policeman and a distant relative.

I remembered the times in primary school where I'd wanted to kiss my female friends, and the crush I'd had on Merryl, the teenage girl I adored when we lived in Australia. It was time for me to recognise the fact I was lesbian, had always been this way, and had chosen the easier, more conventional route so far. I didn't have to keep pretending to the world and myself that I was straight. I would accept my sexuality. Although I felt a huge relief at this decision, I was anxious about its consequences. I was living in a small, conservative town, one not known for its acceptance of difference. The profession I had chosen was also conventional. Coming out would be complicated ... perhaps I'd put it on hold for a while. Besides, it was all theoretical - there was no eligible woman around anyway.

My inner strength to take action about my son's activities was waning. I asked a colleague to phone the mother of one of the boys Chris and Damon had brought to my house. She said she'd begun to worry about the amount of time the older boys were spending with kids from the church, and had already limited her son's contact with them. She'd speak to her husband and the other parents and keep the kids away from Damon and Chris. As far as she knew there'd been no abuse but she was grateful for the warning.

26

Through the practice I was in I made a new group of friends. A gay couple, Trevor and Steve, and some of their lesbian friends Sue and Kirsty invited me to drinks. Trevor was tall and commanding, with an imperious nature that sometimes gave way to show that he was a big softie underneath. He had a huge blond nicotine-stained walrus moustache, and reminded me of a character from Asterix comics. He took no shit from anyone. His partner Steve was cute, small and dark-haired, and prone to punishing bouts of exercise and diet. I accompanied him once on a jog around a school playing field. I stopped sooner than he did, panting and clutching my chest. He made comments about black eyes caused by over-large breasts in undersized sports bras and didn't invite me to run with him again.

Many evenings and weekends I spent with Steve and Trevor, and through them met other gays and lesbians. They introduced me to the Casper's Express gay and lesbian dragon boat team, and I became team doctor, despite only attending one of their races. I was a bit hesitant around the women - their 'gaydars' told them I was queer, but they were standoffish. I despaired of ever finding a girlfriend if they wouldn't relax around me. In the same way I had in my massage parlour days, I mixed far more easily with the gay men.

In my empty bed in the big house on the hill I was lonely. The cat wasn't enough company; I longed for intimacy. Grandma phoned me one day to say a letter from America had arrived at her house. It was addressed to me, and there was no name or return address on the back of envelope. Would she like me to forward it?

How intriguing. Who would write to me from the States?

The mystery was solved two days later. I opened the letter at the mailbox, and read it before heading back up the driveway. It was from Floyd, the American sailor I'd loved when eighteen, and idealised most of the time since. It was my first contact with him in seventeen years. The letter arrived on a day when I was feeling dejected about the lack of a partner to share my good fortune with. I longed to hear someone say that they loved me and admired me for what I'd achieved.

In his letter, Floyd told me he loved me still, and had thought of me often over the years. He wanted to make contact and maybe see me again. He asked after Christopher, and gave me a brief outline of his life since our last communication. I'm embarrassed to admit that I was delighted. Somebody loved me! So, he was male, but he wanted me. He could be part of my life - Floyd knew that I'd been a stripper and a prostitute, and was still alive to be proud of everything I'd accomplished since then. Other friends had died or disappeared from my life.

I wrote back immediately saying I loved him too and told him what I was now doing with my life.

He responded with a page about how proud he was of me. I told him I thought I might be of the Sapphic persuasion, but he felt all I needed was the right man. Maybe … I wasn't sure about this, but needed someone in my life. Floyd would do. It didn't occur to me that my decision-making processes were flaky - I was so delighted to be told that I was loved.

27

Several things were missing since Chris's last visit. My Walkman, some cassettes, and a couple of bottles of spirits had disappeared. I was careful to always keep money, medical equipment and prescription pads hidden from him - this was obviously not enough.

I'd heard back from the woman whose child had been spending time with Chris and Damon. Her son had said he and his two cousins had been abused by the older boys. The police were involved. When I rang Damon's house to confront Chris I was told he didn't want to speak to me. Damon's young brother, eight years old, answered the phone. I hadn't known there was a young child in the house. Surely Chris wouldn't touch him. I anguished for a day, then phoned the number back. I spoke to Damon's mother, and told her of Chris's history of sexual offending, and my fears for her youngest son's safety. She brushed me off. Chris had primed her for such a call from me and she thought I was lying. I'd done all I could.

I'd stopped taking Prozac a few months earlier, still vaguely ashamed of my need for anti-depressant medication, and was now feeling its absence. Despite my beautiful surroundings and rewarding job, I was depressed. It felt like depression - my black bear - had body-slammed me. I hid my condition well from my colleagues, until it got to the point where I couldn't concentrate properly, and was exhausted from lack of sleep.

Slowly, painfully, my new life began to fall apart. I couldn't sleep, couldn't pay my bills. My decision-making around money wasn't wise at the best of times; when I was depressed it was diabolical. The days seemed too short for all the work I needed to fit into them to be able to clear my debt and maintain my standard of living. I approached one of my colleagues at the end of our evening surgery. As soon as I'd told him that my dearest wish was to curl into a little ball in the corner and sleep forever, he realised how unwell I was. He prescribed sleeping pills (at my request), and a three-month course of Prozac. He also gave me a month off work, essential if I was to become well again.

Along with the depression, a deep fearfulness had grown. I was terrified that Chris would come and attack me, in retaliation for telling more people about his sexual offending. He simply couldn't be allowed unsupervised access to kids. I made a statement to police about his sexual activities, in an attempt to have him arrested and treated.

I had a video monitor connected to the front door of my house so I'd know who my visitors were before deciding whether or not to let them in, and changed my phone number to avoid the abusive calls I was receiving from Chris and his friends. Then I went home to rest.

The prescription gave me ninety sleeping pills (Imovane, not related to Temazepam), and ninety Prozac. The downside of anti-depressant treatment is the 10 to 14 day delay for its effect to become apparent. The knowledge that I'd probably get worse before improving frightened me. What if I was to sleep for two weeks - waking to take the Prozac so I'd get better - then wake fully with no depression? I had enough sleeping pills to be able to do that, and a whole month off work. Just like the stupid decision to take sleeping pills when I was at Wellington Women's Hospital, it seemed like the best idea I'd ever had.

28

I changed the sheets on my bed, and aired the house out while I had a shower. All the doors and windows had new security locks, so I could keep them open part-way and not fear unwanted company - and prepared for my long sleep. I hoped ninety Imovane would be enough for two weeks. If it weren't, I'd get some more. I had my own prescription pads, after all.

I told Floyd in a long letter that I was unwell, but didn't elaborate. I didn't want him to think I was a nutcase and abandon me.

At two that afternoon I went to bed, a pile of books, a glass of water, and my pills by my side. I kept Floyd's second letter, the one where he told me how proud he was of me, under the pillow. I read it several times a day. The first day of my big sleep, I used three Imovane, one at a time, only taking another when I woke from the last … and two Prozac. I ate nothing. The second day I took ten Imovane, two Prozac and no food. I cleared the mail, fed the cat, picked some flowers, and snuggled down into my bed after taking another few pills.

The anticipation of sleep was exquisite. The feel of the stiff, cool cotton sheets against my skin, the softness of the feather pillow beneath my face, these were the most sensual of experiences. Every moment I was out of my bed, I longed for it, for sleep, oblivion, the death of fear. I loved, and lived for, unconsciousness.

The ninety Imovane lasted less than a week. I couldn't

tell if I was depressed still because I didn't want to be awake long enough to find out. I guess my desire for oblivion gave its own answer, one I was too sick and sedated to understand. I called a taxi and rode to a pharmacy, where I collected, on a script made out for myself, a further one hundred sleeping pills. I was being careful not to repeat the mistakes of the past. I didn't prescribe myself Temazepam - that would have been stupid, unthinkable. In my confused, overloaded, irrational state I couldn't see that what I was doing was just as stupid and unthinkable. I took some of the pills as soon as I got home, and had a shower - my first in several days. The contours of my body felt different, smoother and flatter. It was not surprising. I was hardly eating anything.

Still, the sleep was what I needed. It cuddled me, kept me safe and banished all my worries. It was a nuisance to wake, to have to press all the little white tablets from their foil cocoons, to swallow them, along with bits of their silvery jackets. It was a hassle to be reminded of the real world, a few metres outside my room, where anything could be happening.

My second Imovane script lasted four days. The third script for a hundred lasted three, the fourth, only two.

I was sleeping at least twenty hours every day. The remaining four I watched TV, spoke to Lucy, a nurse friend who sometimes came over for coffee, or to coax me to eat. Or I did housework. The dusting still needed doing and the cat had to be fed. The letterbox needed clearing. I couldn't concentrate enough to do the cryptic crosswords. My vision was so blurry I couldn't even read the news headlines. It didn't matter though; nothing was as appealing as my sheets, my duvet, and my pillow. My universe was centred on my bed. The sleep was a kind of death, and I embraced it.

I saw Paul and Paulie, who sometimes stayed in the house while I slept. In one of my lucid moments I remember Paulie asking me why I was always wearing what he called my "ugly dress" - the green and blue dressing gown that was all I wore any more. I no longer left the house. Paul picked up a couple of prescriptions for me, Lucy another couple. I was careful to let no one know that other people were getting Imovane for me too. No one, not even me, knew how many pills I was getting through. I think my friends thought it was depression making me sleep so much. None of them would willingly have collaborated in my abuse had they known how many pills I was taking. I played my hand too carefully for that. Despite spending most of my life unconscious, I was alert and self-protective enough when awake to ensure my supply of Imovane.

Lucy took me to Taupo for a few days rest. I slept on the way there in the car, waking to see snow on the Desert Road, and being unable to get back to sleep. I didn't want Lucy to see how many pills I was taking - now around seventy-five a day. I had to wait to get to her place before taking more tablets in the loo. She would have been horrified at my behaviour, and might have refused to help me get more pills if she'd realised how fast I was going through them.

Hunting for clues on depression some months later I came across the following lines which echoed my feelings at this time:

> In moods of heavy despondency, one feels as if it would be delightful to sink down in some quiet spot, and lie there forever, letting the soil gradually accumulate and form a little hillock over us, and the grass and perhaps flowers gather over it. At such times, death is too much of an event to be wished for; we have not the spirits to encounter it; but choose to pass out of existence in this sluggish way.

Nathaniel Hawthorne, *The American Notebooks*

In a way, I had passed out of existence and into a new type of life. I was comfortably, perpetually numb.

29

For six weeks I was off work. I have no recollection of most of this time; my life spent unconscious or searching for pills. Over subsequent months I learned of the number of people who came to visit me during those times. I would wake, make them a tea or coffee, and fall asleep while they were speaking to me. Several of them had to let themselves out when they couldn't wake me again. I am surprised that no one forcibly took me to another doctor for treatment, but also grateful that my friends kept an eye on me, and would eventually have sought help for me if I hadn't finally sorted myself out.

Clayton, who'd been my lover for a few months in my final year at Med School, planned to visit the Coast for a couple of days and tried to get hold of me. He rang my work, and was told I was away sick. The nurse wouldn't give him my phone number. He called another friend of his - a GP I worked with, got my number from her, and phoned me. I told him I was too sick for visitors, and rolled over to sleep some more.

At this stage I was taking a hundred sleeping tablets each day, and had only brief periods of lucidity. My friend Lucy spent nights at my house, watching me. She was supportive and helpful, caring for me not because she approved of my behaviour - she stayed solely because she thought it was the decent thing to do. My gratitude to her is immense, and inexpressible.

Late the next night while I was semi-conscious, Clayton

knocked at the door. He lived in a South Island town and was passing through on his way to a sporting event. He was drunk and looking for a bed. I don't know who gave him my address. Lucy opened the door. She told him I was very sick, didn't want visitors, and he should find himself a motel. He pushed past her, saying he was a doctor, and wanted to see me himself. Lucy showed him to my room. I apparently told him since it was so late he could sleep next door in Paulie's room, or in my bed. He chose the latter, and took it for an invitation it wasn't. Despite the fact I was largely incoherent, barely conscious and depressed, the gallant doctor climbed aboard and fucked me, without using a condom. My memory of the event is patchy, but in no way was the sex consensual; I was too sick to know what was happening. He slept with me that night, going the following morning to a colleague's house and boasting to her that he'd bonked me. He also told her I was off my face on drugs, and hoped I wasn't seeing patients - charming of a man with no conscience to worry about other people's safety.

Clayton told her I'd been all over him - had begged him for sex. He told her he was worried about the drugged state I had been in. I don't recall begging for sex. All I remember is wiping his stickiness off me the following morning, as the memory of the night's activity returned. What a stud; what a friend; what a caring health professional Doctor C was. I was upset, but so ashamed of the state I had been in, that I felt unable to make a complaint to the police or the Medical Council: who wants to hear an addict complain about a rapist?

This man is still a practising doctor. I hope he treats his patients better than he does his sick 'friends'. To add insult to injury, when I did track him down a fortnight later, Clayton refused to have an HIV test or swabs to show he was clear of any sexually transmitted infection.

The incident with Clayton shook me up. Lucy was distressed and apologetic that she'd let him get past her. I had put the two of us in danger by my actions, and had to sort myself out.

I set a date to return to work, and began a huge effort to clean up my act. Ten days before I was due to resume practice seemed like an appropriate time to kick my sleeping pill habit. I went cold turkey, and spent three nights sleepless, pacing, and trying to read. On the fourth I could slumber again: it was a deep, refreshing sleep, with an unbelievably pure quality - one that needed no assistance - one with dreams, and with a natural end. It was the best sleep I'd had in ages. I have never taken another sleeping pill.

30

In my lost weeks I had slimmed down by 22 kilograms - part of this from starvation, the rest due to the loss of muscle tissue from prolonged immobility.

The Prozac was working its magic and I saw the world as a place of hope again. During my drugged period I had borrowed several thousand dollars from friends, and sent $5000 of this to Floyd, so he could come to New Zealand and make my life complete. The balance paid bills and enabled me to keep myself solvent despite the time I'd been sick and unable to work. I had no immediate means to repay it.

Now that I felt well, I approached my job with vigour again, not appreciating how stupid I'd been, and how lucky I was to still be able to practise medicine. I was working sixty hours a week, and still finding it hard to clear my debts.

I applied for a job that would allow me to work fewer hours for the same money. I travelled to Auckland to be interviewed for the position of Medical Director of a clinic about to open on the Coast. I knew the position was mine when I looked across the aisle of the plane on which I was travelling to Auckland. Seated opposite me was Ken Blackburn, an actor who had recently finished playing the role of a Medical Director on Shortland Street. What better omen could I have had?

I started my new position the week after Floyd arrived. Over the years since I'd last seen him, Floyd had blossomed into a tall, good-looking man - in my mind. Reality was not so kind. His letters had portrayed him as sensitive and intelligent

- a man who shared my interest in physics and literature. The photos he'd sent me always showed him far in the background, the camera poorly focused.

The man who came off the plane was ugly, short and bigoted, with an intense hatred towards "niggers", "faggots" and me. I fell as short of his expectations as he did of mine. I had too much invested - in terms of money and emotion - to send him straight back to the States. We slept together - months of horny letters had produced a passion we would never have found otherwise. The sex was athletic, but in no way made me feel straight.

I was now ready to say goodbye to my heterosexual side, especially when I found myself sneaking around to see a woman who became my lover while Floyd was still living with me. His discovery of a love-bite on my neck, after I'd spent the day in bed with Sue, brought our relationship to an angry conclusion. The reciprocality and gentleness of sex with Sue convinced me that I was lesbian.

I spent that night terrified in a downstairs bedroom with the dressing table pulled across the door. Floyd was playing an Alice Cooper track 'Only Got Time To Kill' while he stormed through the house screaming "Goddamn!" at the top of his voice, and hammering on my door. I spent part of the night on the phone to Paulie's dad, giving him updates on the situation, but telling him not to come over to my house. I felt too dumb to call the police.

It was time for Floyd to go home. We'd lived together for four months, with neither of us willing to admit our relationship was a mistake. I didn't see him off at the airport.

It had been a year of loss.

More was looming.

31

Paulie was staying for the weekend, and was playing on the computer in the study while I read a novel in the bath. I liked to soak as long as possible, it was a comforting place to be. He was talking to himself as he often did while playing games, and I was only vaguely aware of his chattering. It was around lunchtime, and I called out to him to ask if he was hungry yet.

"I'm all right, Mum, but the man might be hungry."

"What man, sweetheart?"

"The man playing on the computer with me."

"Paulie, is there a man in the house?" I hadn't heard anyone knock, and was horrified that he might have let someone in.

"Yes, but it's okay. He told me he's a nice man."

"Is there somebody there?" I shouted, now really worried, and reaching for a towel.

"Um, yeah, sorry. I didn't mean to scare you." It was a man's voice, coming from the study. Unbelievable. I pushed the door closed and hauled my clothes on. Fully dressed, I walk down the hallway to the study.

"Who the hell are you?" I'd never seen this person before, a man in his 40s, and here he was sitting in my house, happy as anything, playing computer games in the darkened room with my disabled son.

"How long have you been here?"

"About quarter of an hour. I'm one of Chris and Damon's

friends. Thought I'd pop in on my way past. I've just been to a Scout jamboree at Tatum Park. Chris told me where you lived, so I thought I'd say "Hi."

The man made my skin crawl. Something about him felt sleazy and unsafe. I wondered why he'd felt the need to tell Paulie he was a nice man. He seemed to notice my discomfort, and excused himself after giving me his business card. It described him as a computer consultant. After he left I made Paulie promise to never, ever let anyone in the house without telling me. Weeks later I found the man's name in Deborah Coddington's book of paedophiles and sex offenders, a book which I believe serves a useful purpose. It's not the 'outing' of paedophiles that labels them for life; it's the decision they took in the first place to offend. The community has the right to be protected from their wilful activities.

I finally came out as a lesbian to my straight friends and workmates. This was hastened greatly by Sue turning up drunk at my work, offering to see patients, and calling me "darling" in front of all the staff. The timing was superb. Devotion, the annual Wellington Gay, Lesbian and Transgender Festival was about to happen. I took part in the parade, sitting at the head of the dragon boat float.

At last I felt like I really belonged somewhere.

32

My 'coming out' was not a big deal. I didn't sit my family or friends down to tell them, I just introduced them to whichever woman I was going out with at the time, and expected them to get the gist. They did. One or two friends asked me why it had taken me so long to realise the truth about myself. I didn't think that needed answering. Because there was so much other 'sturm und drang' (storm and stress) in my life I hardly needed the extra marginalisation that being gay entailed, and besides, I had enjoyed several positive sexual relationships with men.

Reactions to my new status were fairly laid back, after all this was the 1990s and lesbianism was just about flavour of the month. I did notice a certain reserve among some of my straight female friends, though, not that I was about to stick my tongue in their … ear.

A few weeks later Chris was arrested for the sexual violation of Damon's eight-year-old brother. He went to court and was convicted and given a suspended sentence for the indecent assault and sexual violation of a boy aged under 12. In mitigation his lawyer said Chris had been abandoned as a child by his mother, and had been the victim of abuse himself. I cringed in the back of the courtroom. The court directed that Chris live with me. He moved in.

Upset that he'd received only a suspended sentence, the victim's mother made posters with Chris's name and photo on them, and distributed them all over Wellington. Chris smiled from posters on lamp-posts and glued to hoardings and other advertising fixtures. He was everywhere. The posters included a plea for anyone seeing him with a child to call the police immediately. The woman's action was the lead story in the *Evening Post*, accompanied by a large photograph of the smiling Christopher. The headline read 'Teen sex offender targeted'. Television news picked up the story.

My phone rang constantly and people arrived at my home with the newspaper article, wondering whether I'd seen it. Two radio journalists phoned me at my new work, having made the connection between Dr Roche and the teenage paedophile. When a Radio New Zealand reporter asked me "How do you feel, Dr Roche, about your son's offending?" I could have hit her. How did she bloody think I felt? Distraught, of course, and deeply upset for the victim and his parents. I had no anger towards them for going public, only deep disgust that Chris had abused their hospitality as well as the youngest member of their family. I begged the reporter not to identify Dr Roche as Chris's mother.

Chris came to live with me again, as ordered by the court. His stealing and other unwelcome behaviours recommenced almost immediately. Damon obviously no longer accompanied him everywhere. Chris seemed unaware of how lucky he was to have avoided prison, and said he saw no reason to behave himself now - despite the fact that any further conviction would likely see him locked up. I insisted that he kept away from Grandma's house, knowing that if he went there he'd hassle her for money. He promised to keep away. I gave him a small amount of pocket money, and provided all meals and accommodation. I wouldn't buy smokes or drugs for him, so he was compelled to get some money of his own.

I hoped this would provide the impetus he needed to get a job or sign up for the dole. I was staggered one day when he told me that he was making money by doing blowjobs in public toilets.

Although deeply disappointed, I told him that I thought this was preferable to him extorting money from Grandma. I guess my own work in the sex industry made me see his choice of occupation differently to other parents, and less inclined to make judgements.

A couple of weeks later I learned that he was lying about the source of his money. One of my cousins phoned and told me that Chris had been stealing things from Grandma's house, and making her pay to have them returned. One of the things he took was a television given to her by a friend, now dead. She paid Chris $200 to have her property returned, but didn't see the TV or the money again. Grandma didn't want to tell me what he'd been doing to her. She loved Chris still, and didn't want me to be angry with him.

Disgusted with his behaviour, I confronted Chris. We argued. He denied he'd been to Miramar, and when he realised I'd spoken to Grandma he pointed his fingers to my temple - gun style - and told me he'd kill me if I kept interfering. I had a witness to this - Trevor was visiting, and later assisted me in making a complaint to the police about Chris's threat.

That night Chris wanted to use my car. I refused, and he stormed from the house, screaming his own car tyres on the way down the drive. I went downstairs to lock up, and realised that a long, recently sharpened filleting knife was missing from the kitchen. I searched the house and garage for it, before calling the police to report that a distressed teenage boy had taken off with a knife. The police knew Chris's history, and took the complaint seriously. Chris phoned me half an hour later and said he was heading for Levin. I told him I'd spoken to the police, and reported that he was missing, and had taken a knife from the kitchen.

He was furious. He spent the night at Grandma's, but ditched the knife before he got there. The police were looking for him north of my place, so he wasn't apprehended. I was relieved the knife was never used for violence, and was glad I'd told him the police knew about it.

Despite the relief that being openly lesbian brought with it, stress was coming from other quarters. Depression knocked me flat again, and I couldn't control my tears at work. After crying all over a patient, I knew it was time for another rest. I was determined I would manage this one without any self-prescribed chemical assistance.

I took another month off work. The bank, realising my difficulty meeting mortgage payments, instructed me to put my house on the market. Sue - the lovebiting lesbian - went back to her old girlfriend. The management at my work re-neged on the salary they'd promised, and told me they were appalled I hadn't told them about my son's tendencies, and that if there were more such public revelations I would lose my job. I engaged a lawyer to ensure my salary was fully paid and my family was kept out of our employment discussions. I had committed no crime - why were they treating me like a law-breaker? During this break I decided that my best op-tion would be to resign from the clinic - the management had hinted I might be pushed to if I didn't - and find work elsewhere. I was unhappy in my work environment and this was compounded by both the depression and the stress of Chris's offending. To be fair to my new bosses, they needed a doctor whose heart and mind were on her work, not her hassles. It was better for them too, if I took my problems to a new place of employment.

33

I resigned from my job, realising that I wasn't going to last there, with the hostile attitude of some of the management towards me. I was struggling, anyway - things seemed too hard. I'd had discussions with a couple of other health professionals, who encouraged me to work for myself. Confident that this was the right option, I started my own medical practice.

My office was a small room in a suite used by another health professional. I redecorated it, my gay friend Trevor advising me on a bright new colour scheme. My new girlfriend and I painted the walls a terracotta colour, and hung yellow curtains and a huge Keith Haring print. It was a bright and beautiful space.

I began my new enterprise at a time when I was broke, had no business skills, a high stress level, but all the best intentions to succeed. I had an occasional nurse, an office, a computer and lots of stationery. The local papers helped me out with publicity, and I sat back and waited for the patients to register. They did, in surprising numbers. It was a buzz to see how many people wanted me to be their doctor, how many trusted me with their health. I found it almost impossible to ask them for money at the end of a consultation though - more often than not, I wouldn't charge, or only asked for a minimal fee. It didn't seem right to be asking for money for my services - I have a strong socialist streak, and believed in the ideal of free health care for all. I needed a receptionist to distance me from the commercial reality of the job by asking for money on my behalf. My nurse was only available intermittently - she had a relationship to sort out, and spent hours and days away from work. I didn't mind this - it cut down how much I had to pay her. As it turned out, the cheque I wrote out to cover her first fortnight's work bounced. She still came back to work for me.

I was ecstatic about being my own boss, running my own business. Having survived the sleeping pill episode and Christopher's abuses, I'd shown I could cope with lots of new hassles, and was feeling confident again. There was no depression now - the Prozac had kicked in well. I felt in control of my emotions and the course of my life again.

It was hard to reconcile the way I now felt with the reality of my life over the past couple of years. I had survived a hell on earth, and was beginning to feel invincible.

Where would this rise in my fortunes end?

34

The papers published the strange story of identical twin teen stowaways - Joanne and Sarah Ingham. Their tale of stowing away on a ship to a point off the Queensland coast, swimming to shore dodging crocodiles, and living in the Australian desert for a couple of weeks seemed far-fetched, and provoked a media frenzy in New Zealand and Australia. A Wellington newspaper, recalling my teenage stowaway adventures, tracked me down at my new work and asked for an interview. I refused initially, but was swayed by the thought of the publicity it could provide for my fledgling practice. The interview and photo made the front page of the following Saturday's *Evening Post*, and was picked up by other dailies throughout the country.

It prompted a call from Christchurch, from the man in charge of arranging guest speakers for the Limited Service Volunteers - a group of long-term unemployed young people who join the Army for a few weeks to learn life and work skills. He invited me to be their guest speaker, and I was flown by the Army to Christchurch to speak to two groups of course attendees. The privilege astounded me, and I was happy to help. Some of these young kids were in a similar situation to the one I'd been in years earlier, and I was delighted to have the opportunity to give them some hope for a brighter future, whatever they had done in the past.

I didn't know if it was appropriate to talk about my years as a masseuse and prostitute, so I didn't. I concentrated instead on describing how I felt unemployable until I returned to school as an adult student. At the close of each of these talks, I answered the attendees' questions. One young woman tentatively asked me if I'd ever been drawn into sex work. It was obviously an issue for her, and I felt I needed to reassure her that it wasn't such a dreadful thing to have done. I answered her honestly, and felt tearful yet relieved to be able to share that part of my life. The ground didn't open with my revelation. No thunderbolts struck me down, and the young women who spoke to me privately afterwards were grateful for my honesty. It seems we underestimate the number of young women who are lured by the prospect of making fast bucks on their backs, and later feel guilty about it. This speaking engagement taught me not to fear the truth. The tearful hugs I received at the end of the evening made it all worthwhile.

I kept doing the best for my business - in terms of buying things for it, that is. I wasn't bringing in the money I needed to pay for my purchases and the hefty loan I'd taken out to start up. I didn't know how to claim for all the government medical benefits I was entitled to - other people in the practices I'd worked in so far had always done these things. These benefits form nearly half of the income of a GP; hence, my earnings were disappointing when matched to the amount of work I was doing.

I was beginning to flounder.

Another trap in practising by myself was a lack of peer support during normal working hours, and at nights and weekends. I didn't belong to any after-hours rosters, so had to do all call work myself. This meant that every minute of every day, I was available to my patients. The constant stress of being on call was pulling me backwards. I was getting closer to the abyss of depression, and every working day hurtled me nearer to it. There were a couple of extremely needy and demanding patients on my books. One of them phoned me every night, sometimes twice a night, requesting a house visit. I went to him every time he asked me, as he'd told me he had complained several times to the Medical Council about other GPs in the area for not responding to his calls, and his complaints had led to one doctor being struck off. I didn't want this to happen to me, so responded every time, at a great cost to my own health.

I felt an obligation to try to help this man, who described terrible difficulties he'd had with other doctors in the area. I was different to them - I would manage his care differently to the way they had, and not cast him out as they'd all done. In this way, I set myself up for big problems. At Med School we are warned of the dangers of patients who complain vociferously about other doctors: such people will invariably turn on the doctor who listens to them. I always felt smugly that I wouldn't fall into that trap.

Oh how I fell.

35

The Gala (Gay and Lesbian) annual ball was held at the Michael Fowler centre. It was called an annual event, but the inaugural one ended up being the last. I went along with Trevor and Steve, and my friends Tony and Grant, both dressed as Napoleon. Dressed in a rented tux and teetering on tall, blocky '70s shoes, I felt fabulous. It was wonderful to spend an evening away from my troubles at work and home. I left the ball with a spunky young woman, and walked back to Tony and Grant's flat by the zoo: a one and a half hour journey on six-inch platforms. Just as well alcohol dulls all sorts of pain. I knew that I shouldn't be drinking, as alcohol is a depressant and can interfere with the workings of the medication I was on. Recklessness and self-destruction are a part of depression, though, and knowing that I shouldn't be drinking was almost an incentive to drink more.

I was still taking anti-depressants, but not responding to them as well as I had. I doubled the dose at the advice of my psychiatrist, but this didn't make much difference. The medicine on its own wasn't enough. I needed physical rest as well, and wasn't giving myself that. It's funny how your body sometimes forces a rest when your mind won't let you take one. The gynaecological problems I'd had corrected at Med School resurfaced. I had a constant dragging feeling in my pelvis due to a prolapsed uterus, and I needed a hysterectomy and vaginal repair in an attempt to solve the problems. This was the fourth major gynaecological operation I'd had in six years.

I hired a locum to look after my practice, and had my surgery. The operation was straightforward, but the post-operative pain brought back the emotions of the gang rape I'd suffered aged 16 - the pain of a vaginal repair closely mimicked the hurt of that assault. It reminded me, too, of my idiotic behaviour leading up to the visit by Doctor C. This memory brought me down a bit more, but I hid my distress from as many people as I could.

I spent three days in hospital. A couple of friends from Casper's, a Wellington gay bar, smuggled me in a Gin & Tonic two days after the surgery - bringing me back in touch with the real world, the one I'd been working too hard to be a part of lately.

I missed my work immensely, so ten days after the operation I began to see patients again. Not surprisingly, things went badly. Major surgery coming after several months of broken sleep, the stresses and other problems I'd just survived were too much. The patient for whom I'd done so much - seeing him every night at his request - called the Medical Council one day to tell them he was concerned about me as I was looking "so tired."

The Secretary of the Medical Council phoned me at work the following day to ask how I was. I broke down, crying, admitting to depression, and a feeling I was unable to cope. I was asked to voluntarily stop work while they found me a counsellor and ascertained whether I was well enough to care for patients. I agreed, humiliated to the core. The fears I'd had since the first day of Medical School had borne fruit - the heavies in the profession had been called in, and would surely find me wanting.

36

The Medical Council had always frightened me. Although I'd had no direct dealings with the Council, I dreaded ever being called to account to them. They seemed to me like a shadowy medical police force, with the power to censure and dismiss from practice any doctor who didn't follow 'The Rules'. I thought of them as 'The Men in Grey'.

Part of my fear was due to my secret past. I felt if they knew that I wasn't really 'one of them', perhaps they'd expose me then cast me out of the profession that I'd worked so hard to be a part of.

I was summoned to appear before the Health Committee of the Medical Council, whose role was to monitor the health of practising doctors, and ensure the safety of the community and the doctors who served it. I first had to see a psychiatrist, nominated by the Council, and undergo alcohol and drug testing. I had confessed to the Committee my earlier sleeping pill habit, so they were required to check me for any other signs of drug abuse or misuse.

The hearing took place the day my house was auctioned at the request of the bank, and an accountant advised me to file for bankruptcy as my business was failing. I had owned my house for only 18 months, but I had a tax bill of around $30,000 and no immediate hope of paying it.

As I waited in a coffee bar for my meeting with the Health Committee, one of my support people told me that Christopher was on the front page of that night's *Evening Post*. It was not a sex crime this time, but a firearms one, complete with photograph.

The Medical Council hearing was less traumatic than I expected. It was held in a large room at the Medical Council office. Several people were seated around a horseshoe-shaped table. I knew the man directly opposite me - he'd been a couple of years senior to me at Medical School. The other members of the health committee were lay people and medical consultants. They had my psychiatric report in front of them - it had my complete life history in it - and were kindly and supportive of me. They weren't even dressed in grey! My lawyer spoke to the committee on my behalf, expressing my dismay at the way my life had deteriorated over the past twelve months - the depression, major surgery, overwork, Christopher, financial woes, impending bankruptcy and addiction - and acknowledging that I needed to reduce my workload and cease all self-prescription.

The committee seemed to understand how stressful things had been, but could not condone my drug abuse or overwork.

I agreed to undergo counselling, especially related to issues such as the sexual abuse and unresolved feelings about Mum's death. I would avoid all sedative drugs, would not prescribe any medications for myself, and would work a restricted number of hours to give my body and mind the rest they needed. Random drug urine screening was also started - this was thought to be helpful in forcing me to abide by the 'no drugs' rule. I had the cheek to find this demeaning, but did realise that I'd broken the rules and had to pay. I told the Health Committee that my drug screens would always be clear, as I'd learned my lesson. They were, and nine months later they were stopped.

I went to Casper's after the hearing, relieved to still be allowed to practise, and sufficiently mortified by the whole episode to resolve never to be in the same position again.

Malcolm, the bar manager had a copy of the *Evening Post*. Chris and a friend were pictured on the front page wielding imitation guns. Their actions, stalking one another with 'paint' guns in a public park, resulted in an Armed Offenders call out, as passers-by thought their guns were real. Not satisfied with the telling-off they earned, they posed, gangster-style, for a news photographer. Chris was pictured in the driver's seat of his car, gun pointed skywards out the window. He'd outdone himself.

I stayed at Casper's for a drink before heading home to the news about the house. It hadn't sold at auction so I needed to market it harder and sell before the bank foreclosed and forced a mortgagee sale. I still had enough pride to want to avoid this. It was obvious that I would need to file for bankruptcy soon. The bills were mounting up and I'd just been instructed to work fewer hours.

It was a huge step to take, to actually file for bankruptcy - I did all I could to avoid it. I lived in hope that the house would sell for a price substantial enough to clear most of my debt. The market wasn't buoyant though and no one wanted to buy the place I loved. Despite bribing the Lotto fairy $5 a week, his traitorous balls kept grouping in the wrong combinations. I got a flatmate, Neke, another dyke. It was too little, too late in terms of paying the bills, but it was wonderful having a supportive woman in the house with me when things were grim. Neke cooked every second night, real meals. I fed us both toast, sometimes with baked beans, mostly without. I was lucky she didn't look for another flat.

37

Even spending nothing, my debts were climbing as penalty interest on loans amassed. There was no way to avoid bankruptcy. I knew the process I needed to follow, but kept making excuses why I couldn't go to town to file the appropriate papers in the High Court.

The house finally sold, for less than what I owed the bank, but they appreciated it was the best price I would get. I had lost my beautiful home because I'd compounded my misfortune with gross mismanagement and its loss hurt me deeply. I looked around for a flat and moved into one two weeks before I needed to be out of my old house … I just couldn't bear to be there any more. Even returning to the house to clean it and try to capture the cats was too hard. Fortunately, some friends helped by clearing things out for me. The pain of that loss was too severe to cope with.

The Medical Assurance Company that had loaned me the money to buy my car repossessed it. The value of the vehicle was probably less than half of the outstanding debt, due to the drop in value of imported second-hand cars. I owed $13,000 for the car, which was sold at auction later that week for less than a third of that.

I applied for, and gained, a protection order against Chris. He continued to offend, and had been 'entertaining' young boys at Grandma's. He had to be jailed to protect the community. I laid a formal complaint with the police about his earlier threat to kill me, knowing that being sentenced on another serious charge would lead to the reactivation of his suspended sentence. He was arrested, admitted the charge, and was given a date to appear for sentencing.

✳

Now that the house sale was over, and the car gone, I needed to concentrate on my other finances. My position was dire, but I kept hoping for some last-minute change of fortune. My friend Sharon eventually persuaded me to act, and drove me into Wellington one afternoon in late October, when I filed for bankruptcy in the High Court. The $40 fee seemed bizarre - if I had a spare $40 I mightn't have needed to be there.

Next was an interview by staff at the office of the Official Assignee at the NZ Insolvency and Trustee Service in downtown Wellington, to explain how I'd managed to make such a mess of my monetary affairs. I was terrified about this.

Sharon accompanied me to the interview. I was so thankful for her presence. I cried at the High Court when filing my papers, and she comforted me there until I felt okay to walk out into the street again. There were more tears to come - I could feel them building up behind my eyes.

There were two interviewers. The woman questioner sat back and seemed to follow the lead of her male counterpart, a young man whom I quickly came to detest. He leaned back in his chair, interlacing his fingers and looking at me down his nose. When I began to cry again - embarrassing hiccuppy sobs - he leaned further back and watched me with a look that implied I was acting for his benefit. I had no hanky, and asked him for some tissues. He ignored me. I begged him, now thoroughly mortified by my streaming nose, and he nodded permission to the woman to get me some. Mercifully, our interaction that day was brief. They arranged to publish a notice of bankruptcy in a couple of days, and allowed me to leave.

People had told me I'd feel relieved, grateful even, that the burden of my debts had been lifted. I didn't. I felt bereft, stupid and ashamed. At least - for a couple of precious days before the newspaper notice - the whole community didn't know about my financial failings.

38

The deep sense of shame I felt - confirmed by the attitude of the young man who oversaw my bankruptcy - increased over the next two days. It was early November - a couple of days before my 36th birthday. I spent most of my time in tears. A few people phoned me after reading the bankruptcy notice in the paper. They were all supportive, but I was so miserable - I felt I had lost everything. I spoke to Paul a few times on the phone, always discussing Paulie, and how I believed he didn't really need me in his life. One of the cruellest tricks of depression, especially in its suicidal form, is its utter annihilation of self-worth. I truly believed Paulie would be better off without me. It felt like Chris's life and behaviour were enhanced when I was out of the picture too.

In my mind my business failure globalised into a complete failure of self - I believed I was a hopeless mother, a dreadful doctor, and a flop as a friend. It was particularly hard as this time my failings had ramifications for other people. This time I wasn't the one who was most hurt. I had harmed my creditors too.

It wasn't easy to talk to my friends about my despair. They were each quietly supportive of me, but none knew quite how to cope with the way I was feeling. Sharon had been my receptionist at the medical practice. She was an unassuming mother of three kids, and was often described as the salt of the earth. She had her own hassles - it would be unfair to burden her with more of mine. Sarah was an over-worked ambulance officer. It felt wrong to add to the pressures she was already feeling. Besides, I was embarrassed about my failure to be happy.

Inevitably my thoughts turned to suicide - it hadn't worked for me when I was younger, but as a doctor, I had access to many more drugs and the knowledge to use them to best effect. I was worried still. The humiliation of living through another suicide attempt would be unbearable - I tried to imagine being admitted to hospital by someone I'd been to Med School with - someone who might once have respected me. No, I couldn't afford to fail.

For a day I vacillated before deciding that everyone would be better off if I died. I had a juicy enough life insurance policy to pay all my creditors and provide for Paulie for a while. My will stated that I wanted no money to go to Christopher, convinced as I was he would spend it on marijuana, alcohol, or wooing children. He had given me no reason to change my mind on that. To find the peace I was seeking all I had to do was stock up on drugs, and be resolute in my belief that all would be better if I was dead.

Sharon and some other friends invited me to a pre-Guy Fawkes' fireworks display in a nearby park. They wanted me to have some fun, and maybe dispel some of the gloom gathered around me. I agreed to go with them, feeling a perverse pleasure that my last night would be spent at a fireworks display, in a fairground atmosphere. Guy Fawkes' day is my birthday, and its fireworks displays always seemed to me, as a child, to be for my benefit. How ironic to have this event to celebrate the date of publication of my bankruptcy, and the eve of my death - it was right that I should attend.

My mood swung from gloom to something approaching euphoria; nothing mattered quite so much now I knew my life was almost over. At times my thinking was melodramatic, but mostly I felt a peace that had been absent from my life for several years.

The whole of that day - waiting for the evening, the anticipation of the following morning - held a sense of inevitability. I ate 'my last lunch', an event that turned my Marmite sandwiches into something extraordinary. The threat of death made my senses more acute. It lifted, for this one precious day, the unbearable weight of my problems. I saw the garden of my flat with a clearer vision than ever before. It was beautiful, but I longed for the garden I'd lost. It would look amazing through my eyes, newly opened by the proximity of death. Negating my regret at leaving this newly radiant world was the sense of utter peace I would soon feel. My death meant I would be without pain, fear, regret, responsibilities, and shame.

I left my car at Sharon's and walked with her, her children and our friend Marie to the domain where the celebration was to be held. My last dusk, the closing sunset, the final hotdog, the penultimate day. I was aware of curious glances, of derisive looks from others at the domain. They had read about my financial failings in that morning's newspaper; I believed they were secretly laughing at me. I smiled at them but felt my cheeks flame when one of the local doctors walked past, pretending not to notice my greeting. He'll remember this and feel bad, I told myself - wait and see.

I saw the skyrockets that night as a metaphor for my Mum and me - so brief, so loud, so bright was their life. They had a short time at the height of their arc, then fizzled and died.

It was a happy night, my 'last night on earth'. At the end of the fireworks show I drove to my office and opened the drug cupboard. My stocks had run down - there were no narcotics - the patient who'd complained about my tiredness had needed them all. Had there been a few ampoules of morphine and pethidine in my possession, my task would have been simpler. I had some heart and diabetes medication though, along with epilepsy drugs and sedatives. I also grabbed my emergency kit and some needles and syringes. I walked around my office. I loved it - terracotta walls, yellow curtains, a gigantic Keith Haring (the gay New York graffiti celebrity) print on the wall. I had an excerpt from a poem by Thoreau on the wall - its message seemed poignant.

> I went to the woods
> because I wanted to live deliberately
> I wanted to live deep
> and suck out all the marrow of life.
> To put to rout all that was not life
> and not, when I came to die
> discover that I had not lived…

I had lived - I had most certainly lived. Now was my time to die.

I said goodbye to my little office, to the patients I had seen there, to the hopes I'd had that I could make a success of the venture. It really hurt to pull the door shut behind me; to say goodbye to all the hopes I'd had. Tomorrow, though, I'd make a success of the most important act of my life. I smiled as I put my medical supplies in the car boot.

39

Elated at the prospect of release from my burdens, I drove home and tidied my room, then picked some irises from the garden to place by my bed. They stood proud, their purple and yellow blooms in a tall white vase decorated with blue stars. I opened my emergency medical kit, arraying the drugs on my duvet - such a variety, and certainly enough to kill me. I put them away - tomorrow morning was the right time. I needed a night's reflection, to be certain that my intention endured. I left the curtains open to fill the room with moonlight. Tomorrow I'd be with my dead mother. I'd once thought of the moon as my mother, and still felt closer to her on moon-filled nights.

I slept well, my cats on my bed, a book at hand should I want to read. The next morning I woke, still certain that suicide was now my only option. The depression was gone - pure suicidal intent in its place. I showered, changed my sheets, cleaned my teeth, and again laid out all the medication. There were pills, ampoules, suppositories, a tourniquet, needles and syringes. I poured the pills - hundreds of them - onto the duvet, and then drew up several syringes-full of drugs. The medications I had would lower my blood sugar, sedate me, and alter my heart rhythm - fatally, I hoped. There were sufficient quantities of them to poison me in other ways too. I would not fail this time. I wrote lucid 'goodbye' notes to Paul, Paulie (apologetic), Sharon, my nurse and Christopher.

Despite my letters to the people who were dearest to me, their feelings about my life and death no longer mattered. I was in a space where the only important thing was getting rid of my own pain.

I swallowed pills a handful at a time, with milk, echoing my mother's final act. I injected myself with more drugs, both into muscles and veins. I took other drugs rectally, in the form of suppositories. Enough drugs to kill two elephants, according to the doctors who counted through their remnants and monitored my blood tests and physical condition over the next few days.

I changed the message on my answerphone. "Hi, this is Lauren. Can't take your call, I'm walking on the beach, or something." I chuckled at the end of the message, unable to keep the elation out of my final memorandum to the world. It was eight on Sunday morning. I lay in my bed, savouring the crisp, cool feel of the clean sheets. I then went to sleep, after hiding the empty pill bottles and syringes in the drawer by my bed. No need to make it obvious what I had taken, in the unlikely event I was found alive. I wanted to make any emergency team work blind; reducing the chance they could 'save' me.

Later I was aware of sweating, and feeling dizzy, my mind fuzzy. I wanted to check my blood sugar - ever the scientist - but lacked the energy to look for the equipment. My heart was pumping erratically, sometimes quickly, then replaced by periods of relative inactivity. I was pleased. Soon there would be a fatal change in my heart rhythm, and I could rest. Soon it would be over. It was already dark, so must be later than ten at night.

I felt detached from the processes my body was going through, seeing them as necessary steps towards death rather than feeling apprehensive about them. I wondered how my cardiac rhythm would look on an ECG.

I slept some more. Soon the vomiting and diarrhoea started - proof my body was trying to rid itself of the poisons in its system. I dragged myself up to the loo, not wanting to be found dead literally in my own shit.

This was taking longer than I'd hoped.

I woke again, around 3am Monday. I had a surgery at eight - I would surely be dead by then. My heart continued to leap and beat unpredictably in my chest, but it felt like my blood sugar was normal again. I was more lucid. I rang my nurse at seven, and told her I had a tummy bug, probably brought on by the hotdog I'd eaten, and wouldn't be coming in to work. She didn't believe me. I found myself telling her I'd tried to top myself, and needed a day or two to come right. I then rang Sharon, my former receptionist, and told her the hotdog story. She offered to come and look after me. I accepted. I was too sick to be alone, and despite taking more than enough drugs to kill a brace of pachyderms it was achingly obvious I'd failed in my bid for freedom. I was as ineffectual at suicide as I was at everything else.

People have asked why I didn't cut my wrists at this point, or throw myself under a train. It felt to me as though some critical point had been passed - that the opportunity for me to successfully suicide had passed. There seemed no point to keep trying.

40

My nurse was furious with me. I had let my patients down, and she had to call them up and explain I was unwell - again. On top of that, I'd tried - unsuccessfully - to kill myself: what a loser. She approached the man who rented the surgery to me, a health worker himself, and told him of my abortive suicide attempt. He then spent the morning telling people that I'd had a breakdown, and tried to kill myself. For a 'health professional' I found his behaviour hard to comprehend, another painful twist of the knife. Suddenly I was deprived of any right to privacy or confidentiality. The news spread quickly through the community. "Dr Roche has gone mad - tried to kill herself. She can't have really meant it though - doctors would know how to do it properly. It must just be a cry for help."

My friend Trevor heard what had happened, via the medical gossip hotline, and appeared at the end of my bed. I was still groggy and forgot about his visit until he reminded me a few months later. He ranted about my trying to "turn the lights out." He was furious, and told me he wouldn't visit me if I were admitted to hospital, as he'd "turn the machines off." I responded by vomiting into a bucket beside my bed and going back to sleep.

Sharon and my nurse spent the day with me. Eventually, beginning to be more aware, and tired of the diarrhoea and vomiting, I asked them to call my GP. He looked through the empty pill bottles, packets and ampoules, and was staggered that I was still alive. Despite taking dozens of hypoglycae-mic tablets - drugs that lower blood sugar in diabetics - my blood sugar levels were back to normal. My blood pressure was fine, and the heart rhythm seemed regular when he was at my bedside. I was still vomiting - a fact demonstrated ably when I chundered down his trouser leg. He took blood tests, advised the others to stay with me, and returned to his surgery to telephone the Poisons Centre for advice. After receiving the results of the blood test, and the advice of the Poisons centre, he admitted me to Wellington Hospital, under the care of the cardiologists. There was a chance that one of the medications I had taken would have a delayed effect and stop my heart forever. It was too much to hope for.

I spent four days in the Coronary Care Unit. My heart rhythm was abnormal - I missed beats irregularly, and the drugs I'd taken had affected the electrical activity of my heart. I was monitored closely for two days, and discharged after a further two. I spent my thirty-sixth birthday connected to a cardiac monitor, watching the harbour fireworks display through the hospital window. Sharon and other members of her family, Paul and some other friends brought in a chocolate birthday cake. I blew out my candles, feeling silly in my hospital pyja-mas, and still regretting that I'd failed in my bid for peace.

My practice nurse brought me more news. My accountant - a close friend of the man who was busy gossiping about me to my patients - had closed my business down. My name was off the door already.

I'd lost my practice.

Another loss: after so many, this one almost seemed insignificant. It did spoil my plans to try to work out my bankruptcy. I'd hoped to install a locum while I was sick, to keep the business active over the months I'd need to recover.

I knew I couldn't work for a while.

More news came from Paraparaumu. Other doctors in the area were telling patients I'd tried to kill myself - had "lost the plot" according to one of them - and would never be allowed to practise medicine again. My patients were advised to register with other doctors. Although I can see the reasons for this now, at the time it was another kick when I was down. One of my detractors was a GP whom I'd helped through some emotional difficulties of his own, and had been extremely vigilant in maintaining his privacy. It seemed many local doctors wouldn't extend to their colleagues the sort of confidentiality their patients received, and that they, themselves, wished for. The betrayal was awful, and had it not been for the support I received from friends and some patients after I left the hospital, I would have left Paraparaumu.

41

Some doctors were generous and genuine in their support; the others showed me how wrong I'd been in my youthful assessment of the profession. One reason I had wanted to be a doctor was because I believed they were exemplary people - honourable, honest, and ethical. I was disappointed to find they weren't necessarily; it seemed that there were fewer loyalties to be found in the medical world than there were amongst the strippers and whores I had known. There was less collegial support, and as high a degree of dishonesty and petty jealousy among medics as any other group I'd known. Doctors could be cheats, rapists, and gossips. Of course doctors were not better people than anyone else. My dream of becoming a member of a respectable profession - one where integrity and compassion were necessary qualities - had been naive.

My rehabilitation would take months, and I planned to spend this time deciding on the future of my medical career. Perhaps I'd give up, now I saw the true state of my chosen profession.

I left hospital on a fine day, with a sense that my life had been spared for a reason. It was inconceivable that I had lived through the overdose I'd taken. Although I am not religious, it felt as though there was a higher purpose at work. This made it possible for me to accept my failure as something beyond my control. I was tired, though: very tired, and needed some time away from the community where I lived.

A gay friend paid my airfare to Auckland, so I could spend my first few days out of hospital with Mum's sister Aunty Jenny. Her husband Dave had died a year earlier from bowel cancer, and she was living in a cottage on the section where her children lived. It was a week of genuine love and deep peace, and healed me enough to make my return to Wellington possible.

I was no longer suicidal, but depressed again, and the world looked unfriendly and bleak. The notice of bankruptcy was not the end of my relationship with the Official Assignee's office. They would soon come and inspect my house, deciding what they'd take for sale at auction. Meanwhile I tried to enjoy my life - it seemed I was stuck with it.

Each day I had four or five phone calls from people wanting to know how I was. Janet, a former patient, brought me a bag of groceries one day. She couldn't afford to do this but remembered the times I'd treated her and her family for no charge. Another patient, Deirdre, cooked me some meals, and phoned at least twice every day to see whether and what I was eating. Their generosity was humbling.

Two weeks after my return home, the Official Assignee's office was back in touch. They wanted to visit my home and office to strip the few assets I had, to gain more cash for my creditors.

When going through my medical rooms with them, I continually had to remind them of the nature of my business. They thought all my medical records should become the property of the Official Assignee, and a family's records could be released to the parents or guardian at their request - a scheme that would destroy any sort of confidentiality for other family members. My office computer also held some medical records - a full list of patients, their addresses and telephone numbers, community services card numbers, and significant medical conditions. The Official Assignee's office promised me that before the computer went to auction, they would delete all records. They said that there was not enough time for me to delete the files myself, and wouldn't allow me to keep the computer until I'd ensured all the files were removed. I stressed the necessity of deleting files, and reminded them again of the importance of confidentiality.

While I was in my old office with the bankruptcy staff, Christopher was being sentenced on charges of sexual violation, assault and threatening to kill me. Victim Support called me on my cellphone as soon as his sentence was handed down, to let me know what was happening. He was jailed for fourteen months. Again, the male in charge of my bankruptcy looked at me as though this telephone call was some pathetic show I'd put on for his benefit; the stupid, arrogant little jerk.

The Official Assignee's officers couldn't decide which of my medical items were saleable, and which they would dispose of. I asked that all items they didn't sell be returned to me, as I wanted some mementoes of my workplace. I also planned to set myself back up in practice as soon as I was well enough. The man said they would make sure I got anything that couldn't be returned to creditors or on-sold.

He lied.

When I left, the staff from the next-door medical centre was invited, by the Official Assignee, to value the contents of my office. The competition got to pick through the carcass of my practice. They were then allowed to take any items that couldn't be sold or returned by the Official Assignee's office. One of the doctors, a locum who was setting up his own practice, took my belongings. Over three years later, he still won't look me in the eye.

I have since spoken to many other people who have gone through the process of bankruptcy, and from their comments it seems I got a fairly rough deal. When I lodged a complaint with the office of the Official Assignee, the man I spoke to was helpful and kind, and asked what I had done to alienate the young man who handled my affairs. I don't know what I could have done to get his back up so badly. Perhaps I reminded him of an ex-wife ...

42

God, I was disgusted with them - the Official Assignee, the other doctors, the receptionist from the medical centre next door who kept coming over to stare as I was stripped of more of my assets and dignity. There was more to come. The nosy receptionist from next door was known as a gossip, a fact that lost the practice some patients. One of these disaffected former patients came to me for referral to a surgeon when she wanted some intimate surgery. She didn't want Nosy to blab about her private circumstances to anyone else, hence came to see me. Confidentiality was paramount, and I spent a long time reassuring her she would get that at my surgery.

Because of the turbulent time I was going through, combined with a measure of personal disorganisation, I hadn't completed the paperwork that would ensure I was paid for seeing her, or a dozen or so other recent patients. Without consulting me, the Official Assignee gave these documents to the receptionist next door, to complete. The patient's biggest fear was realised, through the stupidity and insensitivity of the young man from the Official Assignee's office.

A week later the young woman handling my bankruptcy phoned. They would be back in a few days to take my stereo, bookcases, dining table and chairs, all the prints and posters on my walls, a rimu cabinet and glass coffee table from my lounge. I was to forfeit everything in my office, including the computer, printer and various medical items. They set a date for a fortnight later to uplift the goods.

I had been told the Official Assignee's office didn't take household effects unless there were duplicates. I had one stereo, one dining table and chairs. The prints on the wall were cheap ones - no limited editions or originals that would fetch any significant amount of money. Friends had advised me to hide furniture, but I'd resisted. I wanted to repay my debts, and if this would help, then I had to agree to it. I also believed in the fairness of the system. They surely wouldn't take essential household items.

A dining table was essential. They took it.

I felt too defeated to fight.

I cried on the phone to Paul on the morning they were going to come to take my things. He was incredulous at some of the stuff I was going to lose. Paul phoned his lawyer an hour before the removal people were due; the solicitor called me back immediately, not believing that my household effects were being confiscated. He tried to call the Official Assignee's officer, but Mr Arrogant wasn't answering his cellphone. The lawyer was due in court, so told me to stall proceedings by refusing to allow the movers access to my house, unless they returned with a warrant or a police officer. The lawyer would take over as soon as he was able to.

When the removers arrived I stood at the door, and said my lawyer told me not to let them in. Mr Arrogant pushed me aside, saying "We don't work like that." They began to load my things into a removal van. Nobody but Mr Arrogant made any eye contact. I sat in an armchair and cried.

43

Could I fall any lower? I had no house, car or money and not much furniture, income or self-respect. It seemed I had failed at everything. I had no money to pay my rent, and soon owed the landlord a thousand dollars. Not even able to afford a Lotto ticket, I needed a fairy godmother.

A local GP offered me work, part-time, doing her on-call nights. I consulted with members of the Medical Council, who were happy for me to take this small step towards resuming practice. I worked one night a fortnight. I was not paid for this initially, but took a refresher course in driving so I could use the other doctor's manual car, and she picked up the tab for the course. When I could drive her car safely she let me borrow it. Before this, my friend Sharon drove me to all call outs.

Another GP asked me to work for her full-time. This was not a successful partnership, but an exploitative one, which I got out of as soon as I realised how she was taking advantage of me. I paid a security guard to help me clear out my possessions and document exactly what I took with me, in case of subsequent allegations by the good doctor. I was learning again that some unscrupulous medics would take advantage of a colleague's ill health.

Yet another local GP, addressing a public gathering, informed her listeners that a certain doctor - unnamed, but unmistakably me - was incapable of looking after herself, let alone patients, and that she should not be allowed to practise.

A letter from my lawyer soon shut her up, but her comments still rankle. I had certainly been unwell, but another doctor's survey of my patient notes and prescribing practice had shown no irregularities, except for the prescriptions I had stupidly written for myself. I had always absented myself from practice when I was too sick to safely care for other people.

Paulie and his Dad visited regularly, and made me feel loved. Paulie made me feel glad to still be alive. He hugged me and told me how glad he was that I wasn't sick any more.

My belongings were auctioned in Petone, not far from Paul's place. He offered to buy some things back for me, and went to view the goods on the third day they were on display. My computer was turned on, to a page of patients' addresses.

Despite their promises, the Official Assignee's office had neglected to clear the memory of files. They had, again, shown a staggering lack of thought or responsibility. Paul approached the man in charge of the auction, and demanded the computer be turned off, and all memory erased before it was sold. He then phoned Mr Arrogant, and yelled at him before calling me with the news.

What a mess. What a stupid, unnecessary mess. I made my own call to the office of the Official Assignee. I asked for the woman officer, as I didn't believe I'd be able to control my temper with the man. She was apologetic - they'd made some mistakes - but didn't seem to comprehend their significance.

Paul, his brother and a friend bought several of my things back at the auction. They couldn't afford the computer or the dining table and chairs, but did retrieve the Haring print from my office, the bookcases, and some of the other prints. None of them had the spare money to buy these things - they did it as a kindness.

I took time to reflect. Things could be worse. I was back in peak physical health, and my emotional turmoil was settling. My flat was more in order; the possessions that had been bought for me again at auction filled some of the gaps. The Official Assignee's office had left me alone at last, and I had part-time work, so I could relax and rehabilitate.

I determined that the months and years to come would be enjoyable ones. I had wonderful friends, including Paul, who had become a dependable and reassuring source of support. Paulie was healthy, and Chris locked up, therefore incapable of inflicting further public harm. It was time to enjoy my life again.

I had the support of two local doctors, and could continue to re-enter practice at a pace that I could sustain. The GPs who had gossiped about me could all go to hell; I had enough support in the community to slowly rebuild my life. I needed to get back in touch with the part of myself that had made the transition from prostitute to doctor - the tough core that had been swamped over the past few years. I was too valuable to let the bastards run me out of town. I wouldn't go.

44

Even though I was feeling better about things, it still took me a while to feel self-assured enough to walk through the main shopping centre with my head high. In a small community news travels quickly. Some people stared - perhaps they thought I might look different now that I was crazy. Mostly though, people who genuinely cared about my health and wanted to wish me well approached me. Many friends invited me out and made sure I was coping well at home again. Paulie's dad was there for support, as were Ruth and Paul, two local doctors who believed in me enough to visit me, and affirm I was worthy of my practising certificate.

Every time I went through Coastlands Mall, former patients who had heard the rumours and wanted to offer their support stopped me. They knew I was broke, and remembered the times I'd treated them at no charge. People hugged me, wrote me cards and letters, and let me know that I was loved. They also kept me up to date with what certain of the other doctors in the district were saying about me. Despite the bitchiness of people who should have known better, I couldn't leave Paraparaumu and these gestures of kindness behind.

A friend from medical intermediate days took me out to a movie one afternoon. She chose *Brassed Off* as being the most cheerful-looking film on offer. It was a romantic comedy with a serious heart - it examined the effect of mine-closures in Britain. We laughed together until one of the characters unsuccessfully attempted suicide by hanging. My friend looked distressed about her *faux pas.* I laughed about the situation, but felt sorry for her discomfort.

I had dinner with another former patient - the manager of a local radio station - and his wife. They introduced me to Sharon Rayner, one of their on-air interviewers, who asked me if I'd do a weekly medical radio programme with her. This was a wonderful new way to use my skills.

Sharon and I continued our weekly one-hour *Doctor, Doctor* show for over two years, only stopping when my writing and occasional acting commitments grew too great. We covered all sorts of topics on our show: discrimination, sexual orientation, depression, and prostate problems were some of our most popular. It was refreshing to be able to be candid about topics I knew well (with the exception of the prostate problems, of course) and heartening to be affirmed by the station and our listeners when things had been so awful. Our show had dozens of regular listeners who phoned with questions and feedback on the topics we covered. I felt privileged to be invited into people's lives in this way. The radio job was good training for the interviews that followed the release of *Bent Not Broken* too, though I was not to know that at the time.

45

Seven months after my suicide attempt, I felt happy enough to party again. I held a 'Bent but not Broken' party at my house - the name alluding to my new enthusiasm for life, as well as my sexuality. It was the name I later adapted for the first instalment of my autobiography. Wayne, the blond gay manager of the local Burger King store who became my close friend, was there. Dozens of other friends attended, including the Sharons, Neke and Felicity - a woman I'd known for a couple of years and admired greatly.

How do I describe Felicity? She is intelligent, literate, funny, sexy and special. Her hair is short and silvery-black, her eyes brown and smiley, and crinkle-cut - due both to her outdoor life and her smoking habit. She is taller, older and slimmer than me, and shares many of my passions and experiences. She understands my depressions, being prone to them herself. Before the party, I had only known Felicity slightly. Now she appeared as a woman, a suitable woman, and one I wanted to form a closer friendship with. As the party wound down, close to three in the morning, Felicity told me she wanted to speak to me alone. She wanted to see me again. We made a date for later that day, and kissed goodnight at the door.

Neither of us had been in a sexual relationship for months. We caught up on everything we'd missed in the next two weeks. We spent every minute in bed, where we learned again the intense pleasure of intimacy. We had both enjoyed our solitude, but had reached the point where we were ready to have a relationship again.

Sex with Felicity those first two weeks was fabulous - energetic, exhilarating, the best I'd ever experienced. The sexual side of our partnership was outstanding, but wasn't the only wonderful thing. We had similar tastes in books and authors, and we were both word-nerds who loved to read the dictionary. Ambrose Bierce's *Devil's Dictionary* was a favourite.

It felt like the perfect match - and continued to do so for over eighteen months. Although no longer partners, we continue to be friends. *Bent Not Broken* was not only dedicated to Felicity, it was written as a letter to her. Having someone in my life who loved and wanted to understand me gave me the impetus to try to sort myself out.

I had been a successful woman, having overcome improbably huge obstacles to become a doctor. Actually, looking back over my life I am reminded of Jack Paar describing his life as one long obstacle race, with himself as the chief obstacle. It seems I'm not the only one who has had to learn to get out of my own way at times.

Why has it been, when things have become hard, that I have tried to mess things up for myself? Oscar Wilde's words have a particular resonance;

> Yet each man kills the thing he loves
> By each let this be heard,
> Some do it with a bitter look,
> Some with a flattering word,
> The coward does it with a kiss,
> The brave man with a sword!
>
> Some love too little, some too long,
> Some sell, and others buy;
> Some do the deed with many tears,
> And some without a sigh;
> For each man kills the thing he loves,
> Yet each man does not die.

> ~ *Oscar Wilde, The Ballad of Reading Gaol*

it seemed I have had a huge urge to self-destruct. Where had this come from? Before I was able to answer this question for my lover, I needed to make some sense of it for myself.

A month after we started going out together, Felicity travelled to the Solomon Islands on a journalism assignment. I opened a hard-covered exercise book that I'd intended to use as a journal, and began to write the story of my life. In the four weeks she was away, I almost filled the book with a longhand account of my young life. I was hooked - this time on something healthy.

My medical practice was continuing two or three half-days each week. The rest of my time was spent writing, remembering and talking to members of my family to hear other interpretations of things that I recalled. If there was more than one version of important events, I looked for other corroboration. It was really difficult, with the earlier years of my life, to know what to believe. In the end I realised that every participant in the past has a different slant on things that happened, and they all tried to show themselves in the best light. I tried not to fall into that trap myself, when I wrote down the things that lived in my memory. However I knew that I, too, was likely to fail the test of strict accuracy in my recollections. This is why in *Bent Not Broken* I sometimes recorded more than one interpretation of events.

As I had no computer, the book continued in longhand for the next six months. Felicity wasn't the only person to read it: I let a couple of other friends see it, finding that explaining myself seemed easier through the written word. When Felicity bought a computer I began the long task of translating the handwritten journal with its multiple crossing-outs and additions into a Word file.

While this was happening, I was having weekly sessions with a psychologist recommended by the Medical Council. This woman, too, read my journal, and we found it a useful therapeutic tool. I was at last finding the key to my self-de-

161

structive behaviour and myself. With that key I could start to make changes.

Friends who read my journal urged me to try to have it published, as they thought it might help other people too. I began to consider this, but felt insecure about sending my 'baby' out for possible rejection by publishers. Another worry was that no one would want to read it, and the whole project would be yet another embarrassing failure.

Some cousins read the book before I consented to its publication. I needed to see what family members - who weren't aware of some of the more lurid chapters of my life - thought of my story. On their advice, I softened a couple of passages and omitted several more. These were about episodes that were potentially hurtful to living members of my family. Some of them I felt were important to my tale yet I left them out to avoid unnecessary hurt to the people I love. I have since learned that angry people don't look for omissions - they attack whatever they can find and show no appreciation of any attempt to spare their feelings. Perhaps families are the reason that many biographies are posthumous.

46

For my 37th birthday I had a proper party. How could I not, having spent the previous one in the Coronary Care Unit? My friend Wayne bought me a Barbie doll as a gift. He cropped her hair short and nicknamed her 'Lipstick Lesbian Barbie.' The doll wore a short pink dress and had a big pink plastic heart around her neck. It was love at first sight! Of course, given my addictive personality, the Barbie collection didn't stop there.

Over the next year another fifteen Barbies joined their Lipstick Lesbian mate. The real mania started at the 1999 New Zealand Radio Awards ceremony in Rotorua. Sharon Rayner, the woman who did my radio show with me, was nominated for an award. Wayne, Felicity, another friend Barnaby and I accompanied Sharon and three or four Barbies to the ceremony. Although I have several photographs of the Barbies at the event, I'm ashamed to say I have none of my friend Sharon.

Next day was Anzac Day. Driving back home we passed through Waiouru and stopped at the Army Museum to pay our respects to the ANZACs. I heard the name of Grandma's brother, who did not return home from the war in Europe. Of course Barbie got in on the action, We renamed her Patriot Barbie for the day and got shots of her driving tanks, being fired out of cannons and climbing up nets. We used a whole film on the plastic one, that trip. The Barbie Album was born.

After *Bent Not Broken* was published there were many

more opportunities for Barbie to seize the limelight. The first celebrity shot was with Brian Edwards after he interviewed me on *Top of the Morning*. The interview took place in Radio New Zealand's Auckland studio a month after the book launch. Just before we went to air the producer, Catherine Saunders, told me the audience was over a quarter of a million people. It took a couple of minutes for the tremble in my voice to settle.

Other photo opportunities arose when friends travelled overseas. Bankrupts need special permission to leave the country. I had neither the opportunity nor the funds to leave, so travelled vicariously through my 12-inch plastic doll. The Barbie Album includes shots from Australia, Bali, Malaysia, and all over the United States, Britain and Paris.

The most successful shoot was at the Holmes Christmas party in 1999, where our intrepid opportunist was snapped with the Prime Minister and other luminaries.

No one has ever refused to pose for a Barbie photo, and I've asked many. After the first request, when I felt like a dork, I lost both my fear and dignity and asked away. The only person I chose not to approach was Sir Edmund Hillary. Although a photo of Barbie standing on his head would have had great artistic merit, I felt he was too exalted a personage to ask to do it. (If he wants to oblige, I'd love his people to contact my people.) Perhaps my uncharacteristic reserve was prompted by a memory of the Maori proverb "Ki te tuohu koe, me he maunga teitei" - *If you must bow your head, let it be to a lofty mountain.*

Many people have speculated about my relationship with Barbie; do I want to be like her? The answer is unequivocally … *No!* I am trying to be a positive role model for the poor, skinny little thing. She needs a decent feed or two, and the company of less-plastic people. Perhaps she'll find those things with me.

Over the next eighteen months my life was full of writing, promoting the book, analysing my work and myself, and gradually returning to medical practice. Taking the computer with me I spent a few weeks at Felicity's home in Takaka, writing for up to sixteen hours a day - the continuing story of my life taking shape on the page with surprising rapidity. One week of the school holidays we put up Paulie, Maania (a boy Felicity has co-parented for years), and four of her nieces and nephews. The six kids bonded well, and became 'the Farty Family'. Having six energetic kids in the house put paid to my long hours at the computer, but was enormous fun. Some of them, intrigued by what two women might do together in bed, tried to spy on us. Breaking the bedroom door in their enthusiasm, they were disappointed to find us asleep! Felicity's house was on the market and we tried to keep the place tidy for potential buyers. True to their moniker, the Farty Family could be a smelly bunch. Felicity and I instituted a series of fines for smelliness, and this was posted on the upstairs bathroom door:

Big smelly farts inside $2.00; Farting in the car: $5.00; Smelly poos in upstairs toilet $10.00 - GO DOWNSTAIRS FOR THESE!

Much to Felicity's embarrassment we forgot to take this down when an older couple of potential buyers viewed the house. She was relieved when they laughed it off. They'd raised three boys and understood the temptation to levy fines against them.

When the weeks of relaxation came to an end it was time for the real world and earning a living. I returned to the Kapiti coast, where I was working for two surgeries and occasionally locumed for other doctors. It was a great relief to know that not all my colleagues sat in judgement on me and some indeed trusted me to assist their practices. In addition to locums I did several overnight shifts at the Wellington After-Hours Medical Centre at the Basin Reserve. I loved the work again and was once more aware of the privilege it was to be entrusted with other people's health care. I especially loved working with children. One night I had to take Paulie into work with me. He slept in the doctor's bed, while I tried to nap on an examination couch between seeing patients. Paulie loved the idea of sleeping in a medical practice and thought he'd like to help me see patients. He was grumpy when I declined his offer.

Christopher finished his prison sentence and was again living at Miramar with my grandmother. I spoke to him occasionally if he answered the phone when I rang Grandma. I didn't give him my address or phone number, needing to sort my own life out before devoting too much time to him. He was seeing a lot of my supposedly mature gay friend Mark, who kept me up to date with what Chris was doing.

A couple of new friends owned a bookshop in Paraparaumu. Helen and Alan Tristram knew that I was working on a book, and being too embarrassed to say it was autobiographical, I told them it was the story of my mother's life. I eventually felt brave enough to allow them to read the manuscript and was staggered when they were impressed by it and gave me the name of a publisher they thought would be interested.

I sent the manuscript to four publishers. Roger Steele, also a friend of the Tristrams, accepted it. I knew that some members of my family would be less than thrilled about the book, so went back through it, changed some names to protect the guilty. Because I had written the story without thought of publication it was vitriolic in parts, and highly unflattering about some members of my wider family. Roger Steele and I also had lawyers evaluate the manuscript for possible legal difficulties before publishing it. These issues were sorted out before we felt safe to send the book to the printer.

The last sticking point was Christopher. In August, two

months before the proposed launch date of the book, Chris was remanded in custody on further sexual charges. He was picked up by police as part of an alleged paedophile ring and was given complete name and identity suppression. My 'gay' friend Mark, who had been so helpful in keeping tabs on Chris for me, was another of the men busted. It would not be possible to publish the later chapters of the book, as these exposed Chris as a paedophile. We had two options: to hold off the whole book, or to publish the story up to just before his offending came to my notice. We chose the second course, not wanting to be in contempt of court, nor to waste the work we'd done to that point.

The book launch took place over two nights - the first on Guy Fawkes Night at 'The Dome', a piano bar in the heart of Courtenay Place, Wellington. The second was the following night at Paraparaumu Beach in the Tristrams' Green House bookshop.

I had another respectable career to add to my lengthening CV.

I was a published author.

47

My book, Bent Not Broken was in the shops. I kept wandering around bookstores to see it - my baby - on the shelves. It was a strange and thrilling feeling to know that I had a published book to my name. The initial print run of three thousand copies sold out in six weeks, helped greatly by the Brian Edwards interview. I was incredulous. In the early days I thought my readers would be people who knew me and I didn't think there would be three thousand of them! I was in the papers, on radio and TV, and flowers, emails and letters began to arrive from all over New Zealand. The story touched many people, most of them in a positive way. Interestingly, it also encouraged many to write down their own stories.

The only negative reactions came from members of my family. My Dad was the most irate, followed by some of my mother's siblings and a cousin or two. Some of these people hadn't read the book, but were unhappy that I'd exposed my mother's problems when she had no right of reply. I believe that it's more important to think of the needs of the living rather than the reputations of the long dead. Besides, I portrayed my mother in a balanced and loving way. My sisters Tracey and Shelley both supported the idea and content of the book, and they were the only other people who fully understood what our family life had really been like. Their support was more important than anything else.

A new group of patients began to seek me out: sex workers, transgender people and survivors of sexual abuse and depression. I had been worried that the exposure of my past would lose me a proportion of my regular patients whom I depended on for income, but this didn't happen. Every day brought news of another person who had decided to turn their life around after reading my book. Parents and grandparents began bringing me distressed teens in the hope that I could help them to find answers to their problems. It was all so exciting, and a vindication of the book. By the way, I did not profit personally from *Bent Not Broken*; proceeds went straight to the Official Assignee to help pay off my debts. None of the TV, radio or magazine interviews paid anything, and the publicity generated by them served only my creditors.

I have been invited to address dozens of service organisations, and always get a laugh when I warn the men at these meetings to be kind to their sex workers. After all, they never know what guise these women may reappear in; hell, one day they may be getting a prostate operation from her, and they wouldn't like the scalpel to slip - would they?

The book reached the New Zealand bestseller list and was the top seller in some book chains. It hovered around third place on the charts, remaining there for over four months. At the end of 2000 it was named fourth equal NZ bestseller for the year, cuddling up to Michael King's biography of Janet Frame, *Wrestling with the Angel*. I was so proud of my little book. For a while if I saw someone heading my way with a piece of paper I assumed they wanted my autograph. Although a few did, some looked bemused when I scrawled my signature on a piece of paper that they had other plans for. The shame!

One of the management members at the radio station where I worked was involved in local theatre, and told me that he had the perfect part for me in an upcoming play. Kevin Rush was directing the musical *The Boyfriend*. At his urging I auditioned for the role of Lady Brockhurst. I didn't hold much hope of getting the part, but someone must have seen a germ of ability as I got the role. The last time I'd been involved in local theatre was in my teens. When Christopher was a baby I'd gone to drama lessons at Bats theatre, but stopped attending before our class's production of *Seven Deadly Sins*. I hadn't been on stage for over twenty years. *The Boyfriend* had a high-energy and talented cast, many of them teens, and I enjoyed the experience so much that I signed up for the next Kapiti Playhouse production *Out Of Order*. I'm no great actress, but enjoy performing and the fun and camaraderie of the theatre.

I read the script for *Out Of Order* when I was at the hairdressers. Sitting in a crowded salon, my hair purple with bleach, I laughed out loud several times and knew I had to be a part of the production. There were four speaking roles for females. I didn't want to be the maid: that left the young seductress who wore underwear only for most of the play, the MP's wife who wore a nightie for most of her part, or the nurse who wore a towel and had to drop it as she walked offstage. Mmm. I didn't look too appetising in a bra and panties, and was too old, anyway for the first part. I look even worse bare-arsed, so thought I should audition for the part of the MP's wife. As it happened, I forgot about the audition, and was phoned after it was over and offered the role of Nurse Foster. The director had decided we'd manage without the nudity, so there went my objection about the part.

The other stress about my part was the requirement to kiss a man, passionately. At first rehearsal I made my point, addressing the cast.

"I just want you to know that it's been years since I kissed a man." Why did I feel the need to let everyone know? Beats me. It was a few weeks before I was required to attend other rehearsals, as my character only appeared part-way through the second act. I sat at home and worried about the big kiss. How would it go? Would it be all right? By the time we needed to practise the big scene I was so worked up that anyone would think I'd been told to have full public sex with the poor bloke in question. Showing a bit of my bottom on stage wasn't nearly so scary.

The big day came. My victim and I had an early rehearsal to get over it before the rest of the cast came in. I muffed my lines and shook and trembled, only to giggle when Murray tried to kiss me.

"Relax!" I kept telling myself. "It's only acting. He's not going to hurt you." The kisses were gentle, fleeting and brotherly, but still I got stressed out over them. Murray kept reassuring me, to no avail. I'm not entirely sure where the fear came from, but it was palpable. I was scared of him. My tension built in the time before the next rehearsal.

At our next practice I went on auto-pilot when the kiss came. Poor Murray really got it. I went into full auto-passion mode, sticking my tongue in his unsuspecting mouth. He said the rest of his lines with his teeth clenched! I was so embarrassed. It took several minutes before I could see him alone and apologise. He was a bit bemused and forgave me. Our kissing scene was a breeze after that; we'd broken the ice. Murray's wife Colleen directed the play and gave me a certificate at the end 'For Performing Mouth to Mouth on the Unsuspecting'. Just as well she and Murray are such good sports.

I love the theatre. It is another way to help people forget their worries for a while, and is healing in its own way.

My writing has taken off in other directions too. Many pieces of my short fiction and an essay about my disabled son Paulie were published in the United States and on the internet in the past year. Two people have approached me for assistance in writing their own life stories, and my collaboration with Trish, a young woman with cerebral palsy, is almost complete.

A novel is half-way through and is coming along nicely.

My medical practice has had some stops and starts; writing now takes a lot of my time. I have acted as doctor for Paulie's Special Olympics athletics team, and write a quarterly medical column for *Bella* magazine. I hope to use my medical skills more in my writing, and will always ensure that whatever medicine I practise is balanced with other pursuits. I love doctoring, but my new passion, writing, is one that is not so vulnerable to my recurrent bouts of depression.

I am well again, having knocked my depression into remission, with help from Vitamin P (my name for Prozac) and coping strategies which I discuss in an appendix to this book. I know the depression is still there - like all chronic illnesses, it is kept at bay by medication, and usually only requires a big upset in equilibrium to reappear.

I have a greater understanding now of the nature of depression, and see it as an enemy that can be beaten. I take my anti-depressant medicine, every day, and look after myself by getting regular exercise and the rest I need. I am doctoring the doctor, something I'd never thought to do in such a healthy way. The addictions that I have invited into my life at times of great stress are also beaten. Through greater insight into myself I have learned to recognise the faulty thinking that plagues me, and to disregard it. But when I'm tired or down, my thoughts still turn to sleeping pills. I laugh those impulses away now, secure in the knowledge that I have the power to say no to them.

My maternal Grandma is in her mid-80s, and still lives in the house in Miramar that her father built. I love Grandma and hope she finds peace in her remaining years. She was, for Christopher, my sisters and me, the one constant in our disrupted early lives. We could never repay her for the safety and protection that she provided us. Grandma and I still disagree over Christopher and his problems but are learning that our own relationship needn't be destroyed by our different opinions. She is a truly remarkable woman who has been of incalculable benefit in my life. My other Grandma is in her late nineties, and only recently began living in a rest home. I hope to take some of the strength of my grandmothers into my own old age, which I'm now sure will come about. My sisters Tracey and Shelley are both married with two children and active in their churches. They are happy and well.

Paulie is training hard for the athletics season. A member of the Hutt Valley Special Olympics team, he is my champion. Several of his prize ribbons hang on the dressing table in my bedroom. I'm delighted that my suicide attempt didn't take me away from him. His Dad Paul is again an important and much loved part of my life.

I recently visited Chris in prison for his twenty-first birthday. It was awfully sad seeing my bright young son in that environment, and knowing that he worked hard to get himself there. He will be out soon, having received no counselling or assistance with rehabilitation. The sad fact is that he may well end up inside again.

In order to change his life around, he needs to want to. I don't think he does … yet.

Afterword

The beginning and the end reach out their hands to
each other.

~ Chinese proverb

In my last years at Medical School when I was trying to
integrate the part of me who'd been a sex worker and the
new part - the budding physician - I felt I should gain
qualifications in venereology. This way, I thought, I could
acknowledge my earlier career while helping those who still
practised the art of sex work.

Today, after putting medicine on hold for a few months
while I tore into the discipline of learning to be a writer (and
tore up a few rough drafts too), I am back in rubber gloves
(sometimes) as a sexual health doctor, employed by MidCen-
tral Health. My work takes me to clinics in the central North
Island, where I work with people who may have contracted
sexually transmitted infections. These people come from all
lines of work, but many are schoolkids and many more are
sex workers. My work has come back to where I once wanted
it to be, and I am fulfilled and excited in my new role.

The questionnaire I answered at my job interview asked
such posers as "How will you cope dealing with someone
who has a different sexual orientation to your own?" Oh
dear. Some of my best friends are straight. Another question

sought to weed out doctors who felt judgemental about sex workers. Goodness me, I hope I don't have to work with too many of those! The team I'm a part of is generous, welcoming, professional and full of fun, and I know that I'll continue to feel comfortable there.

For many months before starting my new job I considered ending my medical career, but friends and family kept nagging that I was wasting my talent and training. I'm glad they did. I now work part-time as a doctor, the other part of my life is spent as a mother, public speaker and writer. The months I spent away from medicine were frustrating, due both to the lack of people contact and the sense that I wasn't doing anything worthwhile with my time.

Sexual health uses my diagnostic, teaching and communication skills to the fullest, and is the field where my many extra-curricular qualifications are the most helpful. I hope to spend the rest of my career there.

My writing has taken me into prisons and schools, television studios and service clubs, but, most importantly, has helped me recognise who I really am. Writing, like medicine, can be healing, frustrating, unpredictable, inspiring - and ultimately rewarding. Thank goodness I have persevered with both.

Like all lives, mine has been touched by people who have influenced it for the better, and others who have been hurtful or negative. I wasn't able to get my act together until I realised that the only person who could make my remaining years worthwhile was me. I made this discovery when I was an in-patient at the psychiatric unit. I was twenty, and much of my life until then had been disrupted and unhappy. The decision to go back to school and take charge of my life changed my world.

As for the future, I will continue onwards and upwards, looking after myself and the people who entrust me with their care. There will be new adventures and hassles - I've lived way less than half my predicted life span - but I know I'll now approach them, and myself, with a better understanding. Perhaps there will be too few new dramas to fill another volume of autobiography ... I hope so.

I've had a rich life - one that has made me stronger with each adversity. I try never to forget how lucky I've been - each lesson life has sent has contributed to making the person I am today, and I like that person. I'd change very little of my past.

So what *has* life taught me? I do not believe that we are all born or raised equal, but we do each have the power to change our lives for the better. We can be whatever we want to be, as long as we have the will and determination to succeed, whatever distractions and obstructions we encounter along the way. Learning from the mistakes we have made, and taking responsibility for ourselves and our actions is the way to break unhelpful habits and excuses, and create new and exciting paths.

Our secrets destroy us. Had I remained silent, accepted societal taboos surrounding child abuse, prostitution, paedophilia, suicide ... I would have been denying my past and ultimately denying myself. Telling our stories and listening to each other is the most meaningful way we can heal. By acknowledging, if not broadcasting, our histories we can clear the way to create exciting new futures.

Your future can be as blessed and rewarding as you want to make it.

A Note about Paulie

Paulie has been a constant source of love and delight to his father and me. Paulie stays with me often and although his dad and I live apart we function as a family, co-operating on all aspects of our son's upbringing and care.

Paulie's wisdom comes out in the most unexpected ways. Recently he told me about a boy in his class with "Up Syndrome." When I said I hadn't heard of that, he said "You know, Mum. His brain is a bit slowed down, just like mine, and he's got a bit of a funny face. It doesn't look like he's got Down syndrome, so I thought he must have the Up kind."

Battling the black bear ~ a note on depression

I have been fighting the powers of darkness lately.
Still they prevail with me. But I have more or less
got my head out of the inferno, my body will follow
later. How one has to struggle, really, to overcome this
accursed blackness.

~ DH Lawrence

No facile definition can convey the wretchedness
that is clinical depression. Those who have not fled
screaming down the dark caverns of the mind find
it hard to comprehend the despair and seeming impossibil-
ity of overcoming these terrifying and numbing feelings by
sheer force of will.

There is no other serious illness whose sufferers are expected to heal by 'looking on the bright side.' Part of what
makes depression so dispiriting is the inability of other people
to understand the pain it causes. To family and friends (and
even some doctors) it is something that the sufferer needs to
'snap out of.' I wonder how many patients with epilepsy or
high blood pressure are told they should snap out of their

condition and get on with life.

In writing this book and talking about my own battle with depression I hope to help demystify the illness and bring it further into the open. There is a stigma attached to it. After publishing *Bent Not Broken* my own struggles became well known and a large number of people sought me out to discuss and seek treatment for this mental illness.

I have been on both sides of the prescription pad; this doctor has been, and is still, a patient - a sensible one at times, but at other times unwise. One thing I know first-hand is the singular determination that grips someone bent on suicide, and the paradoxical euphoria and calm that accompanies the decision to find a final refuge from *everything*.

Such euphoria can make it difficult to recognise that a person is depressed by outward signs alone - that's why listening closely to them is so vital. Earlier in the book I mentioned the death of my friend Cookie. A talented young rugby player, he hanged himself one night after a party. His death, and our too-late awareness of his unhappiness, was a dumbfounding blow.

What is perhaps a universal by-product of depression is shame. For me it went further, and was a source of my urge to self-destruct. My suicide attempt and my addiction to sleeping pills indicated my desire to find in sleep a kind of death. A song by Linda Parry called 'Drifting', performed by Four Non-Blondes, says it well:

> What a wonderful destination
> Where I am now
> I can no longer see
> Dropped another pill just to kill me
> Collapsed to my knees
> And fell fast into sleep
>
> There I was drifting
> Way out into the sunshine

Expecting to crash but I'm tied to a string
Look at me I'm a tangled puppet
I might be a mess but I sure can survive
But I had escaped it by pretending to die

Like the phrase in the song, I was tempted to call this book *Sure Can Survive*. Parts of my life have been difficult, seemingly unsurvivable. My depression, the black bear, visits in cycles, growling in winter and when the wind unsettles it, at times quiescent as if in hibernation. But depression can be overcome.

One thing I have learnt is that it is important to acknowledge the patterns of behaviour that keep us depressed. When I recognised that I had, like my mother, fallen into the trap of addiction, I learnt an important lesson. When I acknowledged my habit of hanging on (at work, in relationships) until things reached breaking point, I began to understand that my behaviour was lessening my chances of finding happiness.

Depression is a battle and I am still learning to climb back up when it drags me down. The love of my son Paulie has made it easier, as has the love of friends and family. If only love alone could keep the black bear at bay.

Depression must be one of the least understood and most under-rated illnesses of our time. It's a word bandied about by many people. "Oh, I was so depressed when *Shortland Street* went off air for summer." "I can't fit my size 16 jeans any more. How depressing." So many people use the word as a substitute for 'sad', 'annoyed' or 'disappointed', that the condition itself is viewed less seriously than it should be.

Depression is not a fleeting sense of sadness or annoyance, nor just a bad-hair day. It's a serious illness and can be as life-threatening as heart disease, diabetes and cancer. Depression kills people through suicide: so-called accidents at work, home, or on the roads; self-neglect; and increased risk-taking. It lowers quality of life by destroying self-esteem, motivation, energy levels and the ability to have fun. We have become used to shaking our heads over horrifying youth suicide statistics - well, a great many of these casualties are caused by depression.

I've had depression for most of my life. At its most severe it is among the worst illnesses I have come across in my experience as a GP seeing sick people every day. There's no blood test, no plaster cast or wheelchair, no x-ray or scar that can show just how badly depressed someone is. People seriously ill with other conditions may be admitted to hospital, where they're connected to tubes and monitors. Cards and flowers, hushed visitors and medical attendants all show that these people are ill; that they need our support and care.

Someone with severe depression doesn't get this attention. They lug their hidden sickness around with them, trying to be happy and well for the sake of others, who just don't understand what it's like to try to get through a day full of mental pain and negativity. William Styron in his eloquent book *Darkness Visible* describes depression as a bed of nails, which its sufferers carry everywhere.

Depression has many physical symptoms, and has been called 'the great mimicker', as it can resemble lots of serious physical disorders. Some of the most distressing features to the person with depression, though, are the sense of failure and self-hatred that the illness brings. Just as its symptoms merge and dance with the symptoms of many other complaints (making depression and its sidekicks hard to diagnose), its treatments vary in their effectiveness.

An earlier version of part of these notes appeared in an article I wrote for my column in *Bella* magazine. The column evidently struck a chord with readers; many wrote and commented about it. One correspondent asked about depression as suppressed anger and the relationship between depression and violence. Another wanted to know the role of marijuana in depression: did it help short-term, long-term, not at all, or perhaps exacerbate it?

Some therapists believe that depression is related to repressed or internalised anger; that people who become depressed do so because they turn their anger at the world in on themselves. I think this is a valid analysis. Suicide, the end of depression for too many people, is the ultimate expression of violence directed at oneself. One of the signs of depression can be an increasingly short temper, and violence - especially towards children - can be a sign of depression in a parent.

Marijuana is used by a lot of people as an antidote to stress and depression. Some people find it helpful short-term, especially as a stress-buster. Long-term though, it tends to reinforce the lethargy and lack of motivation that are so common among people who are depressed. Marijuana may also unmask more serious mental illness in someone who is already predisposed to it. If you use it, do so with caution.

Getting my story down on paper has been a significant part of my salvation. I have found writing extremely therapeutic. It enables me to put thoughts and memories that are jangling around in my brain, out of my head and onto the page. When they're out of my head I can get a new perspective on them, and can walk away from them if I choose. My mind is cleared and has space for more enjoyable thoughts.

Writing enables me to define my own reality and exercise some control over it. Through writing down my past, I have sifted through deeply buried memories and feelings, reliving my history. Through putting it on paper, my attitude toward my past has changed from one of helplessness to one of power. It's mine, I own it. Writing has been an effective therapy for me because it's constantly available and needs no one else to make it happen other than me. Through writing and then publishing my story, I have been able to accept the past and move forward.

When my first book came out I was terrified, laid bare, open, raw, my most painful secrets available for public scrutiny. But as people began to read the book I received more and more positive feedback. People have expressed admiration for my courage and honesty as they related to different aspects of the story. There is a saying by poet Muriel Rukeyser I like, "The world is made up of stories, not atoms." I told my story and so far have witnessed reactions from empathy and admiration through to scepticism and scorn, but other people's reactions have not changed the truth I have told.

I'm not cured or 'over it'. I write it all down and, when necessary, seek additional help through counselling and anti-depressants. My anger is a fuel for action. I can't pretend that everything is wonderful now. But I am changed, stronger than ever, and know which tools to use to help my healing.

It's not easy for those close to a depressive person. We can be unpredictable, and trust too easily or not at all. The swings from 'normality' to deep despair can be hard to keep up with. Some days depressives are gregarious social butterflies, other days we can barely climb out of bed or answer the phone. We have to re-learn how to relate to people and to achieve intimacy.

Remember, depression is not a life sentence; it is treatable. Stick with us, we're worth the hassle!

Depression, fortunately, can be treated. For some people, recovery can be made without medication. Depression-busters to try include:

- Gentle exercise. Make a regular date with yourself for a half-hour walk. This can be a good time to clear your head, to think of ways around your problems, or just take in the scenery and smell the flowers.

- Talk. If your friends and family don't understand how you feel (a common complaint), phone a help-line. Visit a women's centre or Citizen's Advice Bureau; find a counsellor; see a GP.

- Write it down. Taking negative thoughts out of your head and onto the page enables distancing and clarity.

- Try St John's Wort (hypericum). This herb, which comes as tablets and as a herbal tea, is used successfully by many people in place of Prozac.

- Beware of alcohol, which is a depressant itself, and interferes with the way anti-depressants work.

- Be kind to yourself - you're the only you there is.

- When things are tough, remind yourself that this will pass.

If your doctor recommends medicine, take it. Depression is a lot like diabetes, in that it reflects an imbalance of natural chemicals. In diabetes the insulin system doesn't work properly. In depression the chemicals involved are serotonin, dopamine and noradrenaline. Some anti-depressant medications work by increasing the amount of serotonin available for the brain to use, allowing the normal emotional balance to be restored.

On kids behaving badly

All family trees are shady.
> ~ *Dan Davin*

No matter what you do to me,
I will not give you the power to make me hate.
> ~ *Martin Luther King*

We are all in the gutter, but some of us are looking
at the stars.
> ~ *Oscar Wilde*

The daughter of an often-absent father and a loving but depressed, drug-addicted mother, I am a survivor of child abuse and rape. But I have not been able to escape the horror of sex abuse; my older son became a paedophile and has been jailed twice for it. These things are part of history, they are undeniable facts.

Abuse victims often live in boxes, compartments where the intellect is kept distinct from the emotions and body separate from mind. Dealing with one facet at a time enables us to cope. To move from being victim to survivor we need to integrate these facets and confront the truth - an overwhelming and potentially dangerous action. But it is possible to face the truth and move forward. For me, learning to bring the parts of myself together and live as a whole person has helped. I own my own history, but do not accept responsibility for others who have behaved badly; who have made harmful choices and taken wrong actions that have affected me. I recognise and accept my limitations. It is a conscious action and each day I reaffirm my ability to survive.

On my shoulder I have a tattoo of a dragon. Traditionally dragons are intense, angry, mercurial. It's a symbol of my spirit. I'm a fighter who won't shut up and won't give in. At times in my life I have behaved appallingly and in earlier years it was easier to blame my upbringing than myself. Many people spend their adult years blaming their parents for their failures, despite the fact that those with exemplary childhoods can go off the rails too.

I have been asked if I blame myself for Chris's actions. No, I do not. I am not afraid to confront my mistakes, but I am not responsible for Chris's behaviour. Despite any resentments he may have toward me about his upbringing, it is no excuse for abusing children. The blame lies with him, the abuser. I do not care if the men who raped me had terrible childhoods, if they were disadvantaged or felt unloved … all I know is that they hurt me and they have never had to face the consequences of their actions. I have. Though abused as a child, I did not inflict similar abuse on my children. Chris and other abusers need to try to understand, if not feel, the pain they leave in their wake.

Abusers must take responsibility for what they do. As long as they continue to blame others, or not take responsibility, they are stuck in a position of not being accountable for their behaviour. As long as they feel they do not have to own their behaviour, they cannot grow, be remorseful, and change. It profits them to remain unremorseful - they don't have to do any work on themselves and can continue to legitimise their behaviour. I could talk with Chris until I wear my voice out, but the fact remains that the change needs to come from inside him.

Part of the pity is that Chris is a young man with immense talent and potential. He has been blessed with intelligence, good looks, and an engaging personality. Despite all the disruptions of his childhood and the times when I have not been the best role model for him, he has a wide circle of friends and family that love him and will support him if he turns his life around. He excels at tasks where quick learning and communication skills are needed, and has the attributes to succeed wherever he wants to apply himself. I love him and would be the proudest mother in the universe if he'd make some positive choices to change, and stick at them. It won't be easy but he has the internal and external resources to make a success of his life.

I don't deny what Chris did, I acknowledge it, see it, feel it. I have been in the position of the children Chris has abused. This is why I felt so strongly about breaking the silence surrounding his actions. I used my anger to act: consulting authorities, talking to the parents of the victims, confronting Chris, writing this book. To recover, I had to do something with the intensity of my anger and horror. My anger has propelled me beyond self-pity into healing, through healing into forgiveness.

Sometimes I am overwhelmed by sadness. When it happens I give in to it briefly, and cry. But one can't cry forever. Eventually the tears dry up and then it's time to get on with it. I have overcome too many obstacles to let Chris ruin my life. I feel okay about sadness; the emotion I no longer indulge is fear. For years I was trapped in a helpless, paralysed depression because I was so scared. I was seething with anger about my life. When I start to slip into anger now, I do something - write, make phone calls, turn anger into useful action.

The dramas with my son have hardly helped my depression. The worst thing about mental illness is the feeling of isolation. When I'm depressed it feels as if I am the only person in the world who has felt this bad. I have the worst life of anyone in New Zealand. Fortunately, since publishing my life story, I'm even more aware that I'm not alone. Through my work and speaking engagements I meet people from all walks of life who want to talk to me about coping with depression and other problems. Our emotions are a great leveller. As different as our circumstances may be on the outside, on the inside the spectrum of our feelings is similar.

Whatever my son is, he is my flesh and blood. By acknowledging my anger towards him I avoid bitterness and hostility, and the good memories I hold of my son remain intact. A counselling tool in the recovery of abuse victims is to reconstruct family history. Victims are encouraged to see what remains after the abuse is removed. Finding the jewels in the dust. When I think of Chris now, I try to remember the beautiful baby he once was. Of my mother I remember her sense of humour, her wild spirit and taste for adventure. I appreciate my grandmother's strength, her constancy, the security she offered me when I most needed it. There are things to be proud of in all parts of my family and I treasure them. There is no progress to be made in the web of "what if?" and "if only".

My mother died before I could talk with her about the abuse I suffered. I believe she knew or at least suspected what had happened to me but she was never open about it. I was determined I would confront Chris and get my anger off my chest before it was too late. I know how unvoiced words can haunt and erode. So I sleep well at night, knowing that I am doing all I can do.

Strong now, I am looking forward to the second half of my life. I'm in charge and creating a life for myself that is healthy and good. It's not sympathy I want, but I do want to earn respect. I have survived and tried to act with integrity. A victim no more, I have spoken out.

Beyond the pain, anger, and grief there is hope.

Bent not **Broken**

by Lauren Roche

The first part of Lauren Roche's autobiography is also published by Zymurgy Publishing.

ISBN   1-903506-02-6   paperback £6.99